Gender Balanced Leadership

An Executive Guide

Karen Morley PhD

COPYRIGHT

TABLE OF CONTENTS

FOREWORD

Gender Equity in Australian business has indeed become a very tough business over the last decade.

A few years ago the public hue and cry began in earnest with protestations from a number of business leaders including this writer, that Australia's performance on gender equity was world's worst practice amongst developed nations. Has much changed since that time? Dr Karen Morley's new book entitled "Gender Balanced Leadership: an Executive Guide" gives us a timely reminder of where our performance has reached and not, unfortunately. But more importantly on ways to improve it.

It only takes reaching the second paragraph of Karen's book to be greeted with a salutary statement: "Rather than improving, women's representation on boards and top teams in the mid 2000s has plateaued or decreased, a situation widespread across developed nations." A sense of optimism and humour might perhaps make one conclude that at least we haven't gone backwards internationally.

But the opportunity of greater workplace harmony and productivity from improving our record on gender has not yet been reaped, and not by any stretch of the imagination. That said, and being an economist and statistician by training, the situation does give cause for optimism. In terms of Australia's median performance, it is arguable that we haven't moved up significantly on average in recent years – as Karen notes section 5.2 that "62% of ASX200 organizations do not have any women on their executive teams".

Many leading mining, resources, manufacturing and engineering companies form the list of usual suspects in this regard. But the positive variance above a somewhat stable but disappointing median has most certainly improved. There are a number of exemplary leaders and organizations whose gender performance has grown positively through conscious and sustainable commitment and actions by Boards and

CEOs over the last decade. Consulting the Australian Sex Discrimination Commissioner's Male Champions of Change list reveals over twenty of them. You will find a comparable list of ten companies on the 'Women on Boards' Traffic Light list. Green lights there include the four big banks and Telstra, which are some of our largest national companies, and where systemic change is not easy to achieve. That fact alone gives us hope every other organization in Australia should be able to lift its gender performance.

Many readers of these opening words may be inclined to think to themselves 'well that's all fine and dandy, but I don't work for any of those companies, and its really tough to get any traction on progressing gender equity in my organization.'

My advice to these men and women is to read on and complete Karen's excellent book. Within "Gender Balanced Leadership", you will find a practical guide to help turn your organization around. Karen has analysed the practices and thoughts of the exemplars in Australia and overseas, and has extracted a comprehensive analysis of how to benchmark the strengths and weaknesses of your company, the types of arguments and myths that you will encounter, and how to manage them. Each chapter provides some valuable tips and suggestions, and there are useful box summaries at the end of each chapter to remind yourself of the key success factors.

In a way the theory is simple, but the practice is very hard. But this book saves the reader a lot of time by starting with the right short list of best and sustainable practices, reflecting the trial and error approaches of those we now call gender exemplars.

So that's a great set of productive short cuts from the best in the business.

Karen starts with "Leadership Visibility and Direction". That is always the best place to commence – not only the CEO, but the Senior Executive team and the Board (if you have one). In fact those seeking an organizational turnaround are asked to start with the sine qua non of achieving gender progress – those at the very top. If you cant achieve mindset change and progress at that level, it probably isn't going to happen, and at least you will know that. The best subsequent choice may be to vote with your feet and go marching out the door, and leave enough evidence in your exit interview as to why.

Australian engagement scores show 25% of organizations are positive about their workplace and their jobs. Another 60% have many attributes of positive engagement, and are on the way up. The top quarter all have gender balance as an attribute, even if the journey there is not yet finished. So use Karen's guide to test out where your leadership stands on gender, and how moveable it is, or is likely to be in the near term. She provides the key business studies on the net benefits of gender equity that you can show your top team, together with quotes and scorecards from top CEOs who have been determined to make a difference on gender, and have. It may be that you have only one potential role model in the top team. It's worth starting there with that person as your firm's pilot study sponsor to show the others what is possible. Karen shows the key targets, actions, advocacy and performance indicators you should choose and seek to advance as long as you deduce part of your firm is positive on having more women in the firm and its leadership roles.

If your leadership's early scorecard on gender gives cause for reasonable optimism, the later chapters of Karen's book will help you go further.

Having an inclusive culture is critical. So many gender commitments look great at the very top, only to be later dissembled and buried by middle management. Having a cultural compass that reads where the green lights on gender are within, and those that are red, is critical. Most medium sized organizations have a diverse set of characteristics that approximate mainstream Australian society. That's the norm. So the key isn't to get diversity, rather its to get it working by kick starting inclusiveness in top and mid level leadership by strategies and actions aimed at bringing those diverse differences together for greater cohesion and higher productivity as a result.

Karen outlines a number of key leaders on successful inclusiveness, including the famous motorcycle company, Harley Davidson. I visited Hartley Davidson whilst at Business School in the late 1990s and was left with a feeling that their Board and top management team all looked like their (then) customers. So clearly a lot has changed, except you will not be surprised that its new millennium customer base has swung toward women as well.

Advocacy is critical in developing an inclusive culture and Karen sets out the latest list of gender myths you might encounter and how to answer and tackle them. The end of Chapter Three opens up a discussion of the most insidious adversary of progressing along a positive path for greater gender equity – unconscious bias. There are two schools of academic thought as to whether this form of bias can be changed or not. But one thing is for certain – it can be outed first, after which you will have a much better chance of changing it. Focus Karen's ideas on tackling unconscious bias towards those in your company who have daughters, for example.

Chapter Four moves to Work Practices. One of the greatest risk points for high potential women to fall away from participating in top leadership roles, can occur when they take a period of maternity leave. Karen starts this section with a range of positive actions a firm can make to support women during this time, and so reduce this risk of key employee loss. And that's followed by many other systemic challenges you might face in reshaping your work practices to balance up realisation of your gender potential.

Chapter Five addresses the three most critical human resources processes in delivering greater access to women with their careers – talent identification and development; performance management; and fairer rewards from equal exertion and efforts on the job. The suggestions made are developed from other business best practices that Karen has observed and researched, and for those reasons are very powerful. Mentoring and sponsorship are important, but so is knowing when to be more proactive in your own best interests. There are many useful tips on managing all of these.

The concluding section of this book comes back to one of the toughest challenges that of unconscious bias. How to understand it, recognise it, manage points where it occurs and especially those events involving backlash, and then how to seek sustainable engagement. These sections confirm my own beliefs that successful future leaders will need to be compelling in how they live out their own personal values, but also how they practice the basics of psychology, fortified by the recent research of neuroscience and neuroleadership which show what turns workers 'on' and 'off' on the job. Karen has made these lines of thought and reasoning quite accessible in her concluding analyses of the last chapter.

In conclusion, this is an excellent book to help any aspiring executive pursue better performance with their career by showing adroitness and adeptness in advancing the presence and transparency of gender equity in their employers of choice. I believe strongly those people will win the day, but an already tough battle wages on, and it needs some more enlightened practices in order to make further advances. You don't have to go much further than Karen's fine new book "Gender Balanced leadership" to find them, and I believe that you will also find what lies within its covers, will serve you well.

Peter Wilson AM Chairman
Australian Human Resources Institute

1.

INTRODUCTION

"The case for greater gender balance is obvious for Australian leaders. The opportunity to leverage untapped talent, and the productivity imperative, means that gender should be on the national agenda for years to come. There is just no justification for not... 'getting in the game'."

~ Michael Smith, CEO, ANZ Banking Group *

What does it take to change the representation of women in leadership? While many executives are keen to achieve gender balance, knowing what to do, and when, is not always clear. This book is designed to share evidence-based insights about how to successfully achieve leadership gender balance.

ORGANISATIONS CONTINUE to grapple with low levels of representation of women in leadership positions, despite more than 40 years focusing on equal opportunity and diversity initiatives. Neither legislation nor significant investment have created the change sought.

Rather than improving, women's representation on boards and top teams in the mid-2000s plateaued or decreased, a situation widespread across developed nations. It has been claimed previously that it is simply a matter of time before women have equal representation, but current experience and projections don't bear that out.

The difficulty of making real progress comes down to the challenges of changing gender stereotypes. Gender stereotypes are categorical judgments we make about the characteristics and potential of individuals based on their gender and lie at the heart of discrimination at work. Stereotypes are deeply, often implicitly held, and difficult but not impossible to change.

If your organization has set gender diversity targets and/or programs, this book will help you:

- ✓ **Better understand** what gender diversity means for managers and organizations,
- ✓ **Provide evidence** on what gender balance contributes to organizational performance,
- ✓ **Identify how** to improve the gender balance of senior roles in your organization,
- ✓ **Understand** what gets in the way of achieving gender diversity results,
- ✓ **Understand more** about conscious and unconscious beliefs and their role in change, and
- ✓ **Focus** your actions to achieve the best results.

The book is divided into five main chapters: Each chapter begins with a short review of your own organization's status, to help keep you focused on what's needed next:

2.   Leadership visibility and direction,

3. Building an inclusive culture,

4. Work practices,

5. Fair talent and performance management, and

6. Taking action.

The chapters summarize the relevant evidence about gender balance at work. What are best practice organizations doing, and what results have they achieved? Each chapter is a guide for what to do to make progress towards best practice.

Each section within each chapter turns the evidence and experience into a simple "To do" checklist of workable actions. Each chapter's checklist is compiled and presented at the end of the chapter.

Having assessed your organization's progress and reviewed best practice, you can then select three to four key actions to inspire and focus your change efforts. When you've achieved these, you can move on to the next area.

Chapter 6 focuses on personal change. The evidence is clear that unconscious bias is an important factor in the perpetuation of gender imbalance. The chapter provides a process for increasing your personal awareness of unconscious bias. Practical tools are provided to help minimize the impact of bias on decision-making.

The final chapter provides a list of selected references.

While you may choose to read the book from beginning to end, it is also designed so that you can choose the appropriate chapter, or section within a chapter, to focus on first. To work out where to start, use the review on the following page.

Current research on gender diversity provides a source of hope for change. While many of the themes that characterized the position of women in organizational life in the 1970s and 1980s are still with us, more recent research shows that where there are more women at the top of organizations a number of positive impacts are evident. For example

- Women are more likely to aspire to the most senior roles in their organization, finding such roles increasingly attractive,
- Senior women's job and career satisfaction increases as does loyalty to the organisation,
- Organisational climate improves,
- The dynamics of boards and top teams improves, as reported by both men and women, and
- A number of studies confirm that organizational performance increases.

Review 1.1: What is the most significant challenge your organization faces in achieving better gender balance?

Lack of leadership visibility and direction from the top – we don't know what it is, how to talk about it or why it matters (*go to Chapter 2. Leadership visibility and direction*)

Changing a male-dominated culture – we have more men than women in most work groups, men are in core/professional roles and women are in support roles (*go to Chapters 3. Building an inclusive culture and 4. Work practices*)

Lack of opportunities for women to advance – women don't get/want senior jobs (*go to Chapter 5. Fair talent and performance management*)

Lack of action – our actions aren't focused, clear or aligned (*go to Chapter 6. Taking action*)

* Male Champions of Change is an initiative of the Sex Discrimination Commissioner, Australian Human Rights Commission. Quotations from their report Our experiences in elevating the representation of women in leadership: a letter from business leaders are provided as section headers throughout this book, to provide guidance and inspiration.

2.

LEADERSHIP VISIBILITY AND DIRECTION

"I'm most proud that our efforts to build a team that values gender diversity are paying off. It's common now for our Practice Leads to proudly share stories and evidence of their successes in developing, sponsoring and promoting female talent."
~ Giam Swiegers, Former CEO, Deloitte

Focused and sustained leadership from the top of the organization is central to achieving gender balance. Attaining gender balance requires as much commitment from the CEO and the executive leadership group as does any significant strategic or cultural change initiative. The engagement of the board, CEO and senior leadership with gender initiatives is of particular importance.

2.1 PURPOSE

The primary purpose of achieving a better gender balance and a more diverse workforce is to reap the business advantages. This section outlines the research evidence that supports the business benefit.

Review 2.1: Assess your organisation's progress: Is the value of achieving gender balance clearly identified?

✓✓✓   Leaders and managers throughout the business are readily able to articulate what gender balance means for the organisation and for their part of the business

✓✓   Our gender diversity program has a clear business purpose articulated by senior executives

✓   We believe there are business advantages of gender balance, but just what they are is not clearly aligned to our business

✗   I'm not aware of any business advantages

Companies with a higher representation of women at the top outperform those with one or no women. Significant performance increases are attained once there is a critical mass of women. A number of important studies have identified significant business returns from more women: in one study, US Fortune 500 companies with the highest representation of women on top management teams achieved a 35% higher return on equity and a 34% higher total return to shareholder.

Companies with three or more women in management teams scored higher on nine key organizational criteria than those with no women, with organizations ranked most highly having operating margins and market capitalization twice as high as those of lower-ranked companies. More women in senior roles is associated with and may lead to higher returns on assets. Female management style seems to be a valuable resource generating superior financial performance, particularly where the firm's strategy is one of innovation: female leadership style and innovation strategies that rely on collaboration and creativity are a beneficial combination.

An extensive 19 year study of Fortune 500 companies found significant, sustained performance differences between those organizations with a continuing commitment to promoting women into the C-suite compared with those that did not. The firms that had more women at the top outperformed industry medians on profits as a percentage of revenues (by 34%), profits as a percentage of assets (by 18%) and profits as a percentage of shareholder equity (by 69%). The firms with the very best records were consistently better than those whose scores were *very good*.

> *"The big ticket the single biggest issue facing Australia is that we have more opportunities than people. That's the business case."*
> Glen Boreham AM Chair & Non-Executive Director

In Australian ASX500 organizations in 2010, companies with women directors (7.1%) delivered over a five year period an average return on equity 11.1% higher than those without women. Australian organizations found that human resource performance benefits such as increased retention lagged the implementation of policies, and that effectiveness was positively linked to the amount of diversity in the organization.

In a study of US Fortune 1000 firms, companies that had representation of women on their top team outperformed those that did not. This may be because of women's management style and their strong personal relationships that enrich decision-making, therefore improving the organization's performance.

A Danish study of 2,500 firms found that differential performance results were associated with women's education levels; positive performance effects were associated with senior female managers who had university degrees and negligible impacts were found where women did not have the same level of education.

Shifting the focus to men's behaviour, significant organizational performance improvements have been achieved in a predominately masculine context (offshore oil), where hard-driving macho cultures were replaced by cultures that were open to admitting mistakes and learning, engaging in public appreciation, and asking for help. Accidents were reduced by 84% while productivity, efficiency and reliability improvements exceeded the industry's former benchmarks.

Board gender diversity has a positive and significant value on firm performance. More than three women on a board contributes different perspectives, greater collaboration, expands board discussions to raise a wider set of issues, raises issues that relate to multiple stakeholders, improves discussion processes and enables difficult questions about tough issues to be asked. The benefits of more women on boards cascades to senior women in organizations with benefits including an increase in the number of women officers, increase in women holding senior line management roles, critical mass of executive women, women with high ranking titles and women among top corporate earners.

> *"The diversity council is chaired by me and made up of the full executive committee. It needs to be us—we can call each other out and we can hold each other to account. As the council evolves it may expand, but for now we own it."*
> Gail Kelly, Former CEO, The Westpac Group

At an organization strategy level, the power of diversity for increasing customer intimacy is growing in importance. With estimates ranging from 70 to 85% of house-hold purchases being made by women, there is increasing evidence that organizations must better understand women and their decision-making styles, needs and preferences. More women in management leads to better decision-making through better reflecting the customer and consumer base.

Fifty-eight percent of companies with diversity programs reported increased productivity and 62% identified increased attraction and retention of talent as benefits of a focus on gender diversity in a European Commission study. Higher productivity was attributed to improved employee motivation and efficiency.

Seventy-six percent of high performing companies with gender initiatives have systematically integrated diversity programs into business processes,

8

reflecting the power of diversity for improving business outcomes. Nokia links diversity to innovation, believing that greater diversity drives new thinking, new systems and processes, contributing to increased innovation.

Branding benefits also accrue as companies that increase their gender representation are viewed as socially progressive.

The table on the following page summarizes key research findings on the business implications of gender diversity within a strategic framework.

Strategy	People	Performance
How much of your corporate value creation relies on people, brand and intellectual property?	Key talent metrics? Where are women under-utilized?	What are your shareholder returns, your industry standing, and key performance ratios?
Consider: - Leadership intent and levels of leadership capability - Level of innovation achieved and required - Risk appetite - Adaptability to change - Productivity ratios - Teamwork dividends - Percentage of key purchasing decisions made or affected by women	Consider: - Time to fill key roles - Turnover - Replacement costs - Capability gaps - Engagement levels - Predicted workforce gaps - Gender ratios at level - Pay equity - Culture - Ability to meet ASX gender guidelines - Productivity impact on career deceleration for women compared with men	Consider: - Shareholder returns - Industry standing - Key performance ratios, e.g. ROA, TRS - Compare with industry medians - Comparative business unit performance

To do

✓ **Identify and communicate** the business advantages that accrue from a better gender representation in your organisation.

✓ Having identified the benefits, **create a brief narrative** that can help senior leaders articulate the purpose to others.

✓ **Integrate the business benefits** into the organisation's overall strategy. The framework on the next page can be used to help identify the specific business advantages for your organisation.

2.2 DEMONSTRATING COMMITMENT

Commitment from the top can be demonstrated in a number of ways. Assess the extent of senior leadership commitment in your organization using this quiz.

Review 2.2: Assess your organization's progress: Is leadership of your gender diversity program demonstrated by senior leaders?	
✔✔✔	Our CEO and senior executives model inclusion and acceptance of senior women leaders
✔✔	Our CEO and senior executives espouse diversity and inclusion as important values although we do not have a good representation of women at senior levels
✔	There's no obvious leadership of gender diversity in my organization
✗	There's active opposition to discussion of gender diversity

2.2.1   CEO modelling
Gender balance on the top team and achievement of gender equity provide a clear demonstration of the CEO's leadership.

CEOs are the key drivers for the tenor of the executive suite. Research evidence demonstrates that both men and women identify the executive suite as inhospitable for women; being the woman is the exception. Gender is never identified as a reason why men don't fit into the executive suite, but it is for women: the assumption is that males fit into the executive suite, and females do not.

Male CEOs in particular are a powerful force for change. A CEO's demonstration of inclusion and acceptance of women as colleagues at the top of organizations provides a strong message that can help drive acceptance of gender balance.

BP's change of global CEO in 2006 led to a mass exodus of senior women, whom it appears were alienated by the incoming (now former) CEO's new strategic direction. This left an organization with a public rhetoric about the value of diversity without the evidence to support it.

Diversity at the top changes the top team dynamics and leads to stronger business and performance outcomes, and increases the retention of women.

By contrast, Mercy Health's CEO John Ballard from 2004 oversaw a shift to 46% women on the board, 50% women on the key executive committee, 60% women reporting to him and 71% of all senior management positions held by women through his active support for the value of gender balance.

Gerald Lema, during his 2005 to 2008 tenure as CEO of Baxter Healthcare (Asia-Pacific) led a gender diversity program. The program resulted in gender parity at management levels and critical positions two years ahead of their plan.

This success was largely attributed to his extensive championing of the value of diversity and support to the program.

Mirvac's CEO and MD Susan Lloyd-Hurwitz has expanded her executive team, achieving 36% female representation, and has fostered an inclusive culture.

In a US study of 1,000 senior executives, the key feature of successful diversity strategy implementation was the CEO's ownership of women's advancement, including his or her vision and commitment to diversity, and his or her behaviour in ensuring goals, targets, accountabilities and reporting were embedded in everyday organizational practices.

To do
✓ Supply the CEO with **data on the business case,** advocate for change and challenge decisions that may be biased.
✓ Provide **gender coaching** for the CEO to support his/her leadership.

2.2.2   Gender balanced senior executive group

Female board members and CEOs are associated with an increased representation of women in senior roles and with their equitable compensation. Three or more women on the board or executive team rapidly changes a number of key indicators including representation of women at senior levels. Diversity must therefore be demonstrated in top roles in organizations to project this message unambiguously: change can't just filter up the pipeline, it must also filter down.

"Women in leadership. It's just good business. There's no difference in leadership potential between women and men; making sure you can capture a better share of high performing women is better for the organization."
Ralph Norris, former CEO, CBA

A more diverse team at the top cascades a more comprehensive, wide-ranging set of norms whereas a narrowly defined demographic group cascades an exclusionary perspective.

Where there is more than a token presence of women in senior executive ranks, there is greater latitude in gender roles for both women and men, and women experience a greater sense of acceptance, higher satisfaction and optimism, and they have a much stronger desire for promotion.

The impacts of three or more women on a board can be extrapolated to three or more women on an executive team and include normalization of women's presence, women are more comfortable with 'being themselves', there is a more supportive atmosphere, individual women are not seen as representing all women, women are freer to raise issues, and are more likely to be heard, and there is increased collaboration and inclusion.

> *"In my mind, gender (diversity) and inclusiveness is a broader leadership issue. Great leaders know how to get the best out of their people regardless of their gender, ethnicity or sexual orientation."*
> David Thodey, CEO, Telstra

By contrast, low numbers of women at the top increases their likelihood of premature exit; this establishes a self-reinforcing negative cycle where few women at the top increases the proportion of those women exiting which keeps numbers at the top low. Where they work in organisations predominately male, women are much less satisfied with their jobs and have a greater intention to quit than women in organisations that have a more balanced gender composition.

When there are three or more women they are seen as more than single-issue representatives of their gender. Where there are more women, men raise diversity issues, as diversity becomes a group responsibility. Other research indicates that it takes a critical mass of about 35% women before men's attitudes toward women change.

Where there are more than 20% women, men's evaluations of women are significantly more positive than when token conditions apply; where women comprise 45% of the management pool, women's capabilities are rated even more highly by their male colleagues.

In addition, the presence of women in senior positions fosters positive working relationships generally, and importantly provides opportunities for more junior women (and men) to establish positive relationships with senior female managers, resulting in greater retention of women at all levels. Sufficient senior women designated as successful makes that the model for leadership and opens new opportunity to women. Where women are designated as successful, people are prepared to follow their lead.

To do

✓ Identify or **shape the strategy** to increase the representation of women at the top. Ensure that selection processes are transparent and considered.

✓ **Become involved in selection processes** for senior positions: ensure that HR staff or recruitment consultants are briefed to provide a gender-balanced shortlist, and hold them to account.

✓ Provide group or individual **coaching for senior women** to support them in promoting and maintaining their visibility, dealing with the dilemmas and challenges of being highly visible role models and forging new ground.

✓ Provide **coaching for the CEO and senior male executives** in managing a more gender-neutral engagement with their colleagues.

2.2.3 Senior executive role models and champions

Senior executive role modelling sets the tone for the whole organization. Research on top teams demonstrates the powerful symbolism of executives and how they come to represent the organization, its direction, values and credibility. Tone from the top cascades down through organizational levels and signals what is valued and rewarded.

In one international study only 26% of male and female survey participants thought that their company's leadership team made gender a visible priority, while in an Australian study, only two HR directors in 30 top companies reported that gender diversity was a top management issue, indicating significant room for improvement in championing change.

Responsibility for change in gender representation is too often placed on women, yet women do not have the power to make the changes required on their own, and additionally, taking on the mantle of redressing women's status has proven detrimental to many senior women's careers One of the reasons attributed to failure of some gender diversity initiatives is that they focus solely on women, without consideration of the changes that men may also want and need to make: this is not just an issue for women to champion, but one which relies on all senior executives to champion.

The way in which powerful senior leaders respond to inequality in practices and opportunities has a critical impact that cascades throughout the organization.

Commitment to change can be built among senior men when they are integrally involved in the change planning and implementation process; this minimizes resistance and apprehension, as well as backlash against change. Men are champions of change for women where they are aware of gender bias, and committed to the ideal of fairness for all. Australian law firm Freehills' gender diversity initiative is supported by the appointment of male partner champions whose role is to drive cultural change.

The best results from gender strategies are achieved where senior men and women work together as allies to change the beliefs and practices of the organizations they lead. Senior change agents are equipped to support gender diversity initiatives in those organizations with a greater representation of women.

Emerging research demonstrates that visible role modelling of women in authority is associated with an increase in women's ambitions, enabling them to identify with success.

Male executives, through their powerful symbolism, are already significant role models. Senior male executives can demonstrate that there are many ways to enact leadership, presenting a broader style and demonstrating more collaborative behaviour.

Ely and Meyerson's research on offshore oil-rigs demonstrated that where macho behaviours were set aside, mission-driven men who cared about their teams, were good listeners and willing to learn, achieved significant shifts in company performance.

They found that men's attempts to prove their masculinity interfered significantly with running safe and effective worksites. In more typically corporate settings, this macho behaviour results in men's demonstration of a higher level of overconfidence than women; overconfidence in the financial arena is shown in research to be detrimental to company performance.

"It's important that the gender diversity goal is not 'off to the side', but rather that it is core to the business, and managed as such. I am frustrated when I hear people talk about how hard this is. When you think about it, having more women in leadership is far more under our control than most other business objectives we set for ourselves. This is not beyond our intellectual capability to solve. Excuses are just that."
Cameron Clyne, Former CEO, NAB

In addition, the way in which senior men include women, model openness to difference and challenge exclusionary behaviour by others creates a new example and new model for behaviour.

Senior executives' behaviour must be consistent and congruent with the policy position on gender diversity or it will be ignored at best and ridiculed at worst. Best practice organizations are those in which senior male and female leaders demonstrate credible leadership and model inclusive behaviour.

To do

✓ Create awareness of the need for **role models**, identify them and recognise their actions. Highlight role models, good stories, effective outcomes.

✓ **Advocate for change**, assess your own behaviour and become a role model. If you don't know how, get training, advice, support and coaching from someone who does.

✓ **Create a positive narrative** that provides a vision of gender fairness within the context of what the business needs/wants to achieve.

✓ Reinforce business benefits and the importance of **leadership by the CEO and Exco**. Specify what can be expected from them in terms of observable public actions.

✓ **Emphasise the long-term nature** of change and the potential for mistakes.

✓ **Talk about gender**, difference and inclusion.

"In the longer term, sustainability is about gender balance being the right business decision. Our experience with the APS was that a series of initiatives and in many cases, new practices were required to build gender balance into our way of working."
Annwyn Godwin, Merit Protection Commissioner,
Australian Public Service Commission

2.2.4 Commitment is sustained

Since the 1960s, inroads have been made in the integration of women into the world of management. Much has been achieved and yet progress takes time. A strategic approach that is sustained over time, with continuing senior level commitment even in the face of temporary set-backs, yields the greatest benefits. Companies that persist with their diversity initiatives for a longer period of time and continue to actively manage the culture change process report greater gender diversity.

Any significant change process will encounter barriers to success. For example, organizations that roll-out mandatory gender training and awareness programs can experience up to a 7.5% drop in the number of women in management. Such an outcome can be demoralizing as well as potentially undermining of diversity efforts.

Committed organizations don't derail from their agenda because of setbacks, but work instead to adjust their programs responsively and persist with their change strategy.

Deloitte has sustained a strong commitment to diversity since 1993 and over that time has pioneered a range of new initiatives to create more diverse work practices and to retain and advance women. Between 1993 and 2009, women as partners and principals increased from 6 to 22%, senior managers from 23 to 36% and the gender turnover gap reduced from 7 to 1%.

To do

✓ **Keep the issue on the agenda.**

✓ Encourage the organisation to see gender diversity strategies and programs as long term commitments, **not just this year's fad.**

✓ Embed the gender diversity strategy and programs in overall business strategy and programs.

✓ Make sure progress is **noticed and celebrated.**

2.3 STRATEGIC DIRECTION AND FOCUS

The best organizational outcomes are achieved where there are clear plans for gender diversity, with connections made to key business objectives and explicit benefits identified.

Review 2.3: Assess your organization's progress: How well is gender diversity embedded in your organization's strategies and plans?

✔✔✔	Our gender diversity program and targets are fully integrated into our strategy
✔✔	We have a gender diversity strategy and program that is separate from our organizational strategy and program
✔	While gender diversity is not articulated in strategies and plans, we pay some attention to it in the normal course of events
✗	Gender diversity plays no part in our strategies and plans

2.3.1 Gender diversity is embedded in the organization's strategy

Besides clarity of business benefits, the best plans are built from a base of relevant data on the organization and its current status, including its culture and gender mindsets. A thorough analysis of the organization's gender situation is critical, along with benchmarking the practices of other organizations. Understanding the legacy of the past through prior practices and programs, as well as current change readiness, are important inputs to an effective plan.

Strategic and business plans connect an organization's gender aspirations with reality by integrating expected gender diversity outcomes with organizational priorities, systems and targets, and provide sufficient resources to enable the plan to be executed.

> *To do*
>
> ✓ Connect diversity purpose and business case into the **strategy.**
>
> ✓ **Create a dashboard**/scorecard to make targets more meaningful and integrated, then assign resources, work out how they can be a part of the overall business scorecard and therefore linked explicitly to business outcomes.

2.3.2 Leading gender diversity policy

A policy statement provides a vehicle for communicating the organization's position on gender diversity. However, a policy on its own is not enough: other organizational policies need to be reviewed and aligned as they may continue to reflect assumptions about leadership being male and therefore reinforce the status quo. Attention to areas such as job construction, hierarchy, language, work routines and acceptable behaviours are necessary.

Employees at all levels should be clear about gender diversity policy and targets, and understand why they exist. As with other change processes, clear communication of why the change is necessary, what it will look like and what will be expected of employees is critical. Creating a powerful message that identifies the benefits for the organization and for all employees will have the greatest impact.

Diversity policies that lead the field include innovative approaches that challenge the status quo, support cultural development and provide a focal point for the alignment of other policies, particularly those related to talent and performance.

Corrs Chambers Westgarth released an ASX compliant gender diversity policy despite not being a listed company, with the purpose of making a major public statement about their commitment to diversity. The policy sets measures for diversity including targets for women in senior roles. Their policy has three objectives, to increase women in senior roles including partnerships, to create greater flexibility for men and women, and to broaden the diversity focus beyond gender.

To do

✓ **Identify key principles or objectives** to guide policy development or review.

✓ Audit other organisational policies so that they support and align with the diversity policy to **avoid inconsistencies.**

✓ **Communicate the policy** throughout the organisation.

✓ Ensure the policy is linked to your **culture** change program.

2.3.3 Meaningful targets are set

Targets, and progress towards targets, provide an important basis for directing action. Indicators such as:

1. The proportion of women at different levels; in different business lines; recruited to senior or key roles,

2. Pay levels for men and women, and

3. Attrition rates, promotion rates and rates of diversity performance,

are all important for assessing diversity performance. Transparency of the gaps between expectations and the current status provide an important focus for organizations and help build awareness of the necessity for gender diversity programs. Importantly, separate 'women's' targets are not established but instead gender balance targets are integrated into the organization's strategic change program.

GE and Shell both rely on strong targets and performance metrics to ensure they achieve the outcomes they seek from their diversity strategies. Shell used a scorecard to measure progress and in a five year period saw women's representation increase from eight to 32% at the senior executive level and double or more at senior and middle levels. In Australia, Perpetual developed a diversity scorecard to report gender representation across the organization, while Freehills set female partner targets, and followed through with regular analysis and reporting of key gender metrics.

JPMorgan Chase identified targets for retaining and promoting women with training for managers on how their decisions may be affected by gender beliefs: in 2008, 48% of managers were women, with 27% women in the most senior roles, a significant increase from previous years.

Royal Bank of Canada had a staffing target to include women in one of every two positions at both senior manager and executive level.

"We have set granular targets for each of our 70 practice groups, and created transparency on outcomes at this level. At every board meeting and senior management meeting, we place this scorecard on everyone's chair."

Giam Swiegers, Former CEO, Deloitte

Besides clarity of targets, ensuring that these new targets are not in conflict with existing targets is important to avoid unintended consequences. For example, is a target to include more women in short lists for selection in conflict with a pre-existing recruitment target relating to time-to-fill?

To do

✓ Review and **advocate for specific targets** that will help drive gender diversity implementation.

✓ Ensure they are **clearly defined**, strategically oriented and readily measured.

A Menu of Targets

Senior levels

Set/re-assess target for senior female representation – in which year will 30% be achieved (male-dominated organizations), 45% (gender-diverse organizations)

General management levels

- Target **50%** participation by both men and women

- **Pipeline**: succession and talent programs to have 50% targets plus audit processes

- **Return from leave**: % of women who return to pre-existing position or promotional position

- **Recruitment**: numbers on short lists, numbers recruited at level

- **Pay levels**: job points values, pay at level, total remuneration including bonuses and LTIs

- **Attrition rates**: women leaving at level, at age, at child-rearing stage, reasons for exit

- **Promotion**: women eligible to be promoted and rate of promotion compared with men

- Career progression rate: number of levels over period of time Developmental characteristics of men's and women's jobs Access to high profile assignments

- **Performance expectations** of women and men as they begin new roles

2.4 PROGRESS IS MEASURED AND COMMUNICATED

Those companies that plan, monitor and review their targets seem to promote and retain women most successfully. Measurement provides a baseline from which the current state is made transparent and progress can be reviewed over time.

Review 2.4: Assess your organization's progress: How well is progress against your organization's gender diversity strategy and targets assessed and communicated?	
✓✓✓	Our gender targets, strategies and plans are clearly communicated throughout the organization
✓✓	We regularly measure our gender diversity achievements against our strategies and plans
✓	While we have targets and some measures our progress and achievements are not very clear
✗	There is no communication of our targets or progress against them

In a major gender diversity cultural change program, Deloitte established an external advisory council to help review the progress their initiative was making: this brought them a healthy pressure to follow through on change and ensure results were achieved. Not only was progress scrutinized so carefully, it was also disseminated broadly throughout the organization, using an annual report, updates and face-to-face meetings. Progress measures focusing on the tracking of high potential women on a quarterly basis drove behaviour, changing the nature of discussion with women about their careers and other management behaviour. Results on turnover, promotion and other key targets were circulated amongst management, increasing both transparency and commitment to change.

Qualitative audits can provide new and sometimes surprising information. For example, Nestlé's executives were reportedly shaken by the qualitative feedback their audit provided: it found significant disenchantment even from those women who 'had made it'.

Sidley Austin Brown and Wood, a legal firm in the US, achieved a Catalyst Award in 2005 for their ongoing commitment to diversity, which had seen a doubling of women promoted to partnership from 2002 to 2004. A part of their commitment was to ensure clear communication from senior leadership about the importance of diversity to the firm's success. Partners were required to annually account for their personal efforts to improve diversity.

Communication of gender diversity achievements signals the strength of the organization's commitment to change, builds engagement amongst those personally committed to change and creates conformance pressure for those resistant or uncommitted to change.

To do

✓ Create or support visible **accountability mechanisms** such as a senior level diversity council, external advisory group comprising high profile membership, CEO bulletins, annual diversity report (public), diversity dashboards that assign clear expectations and responsibilities to organizational leadership, managers and individuals, and success stories of managers and women.

✓ Provide a gender diversity **reporting mechanism** that identifies blockages in the system.

2.5 ACCOUNTABILITY

Holding managers accountable for gender equity is a key driver for turning the rhetoric of good intentions into action.

> *"Partners must commit to our "people power" strategy and to developing female talent as a key pillar of our strategy. Those who do will be rewarded and there are consequences for those who don't."*
> Giam Swiegers, Former CEO, Deloitte

Review 2.5: Assess your organization's progress: How well are manager accountabilities established, supported and monitored?

✓✓✓	Managers have a gender diversity target cascaded from the diversity strategy that is clearly linked with their remuneration
✓✓	Managers have a key performance indicator that aligns with our gender diversity targets
✓	Managers are generally expected to implement organizational strategy and targets but there is no formal mechanism by which this happens for gender diversity
✗	There is no connection between the organization's gender diversity strategy and targets, and the expectations of managers

2.5.1 Manager accountability aligned with diversity strategy

Performance accountabilities are used by organizations to shape and drive behaviour and outcomes. This is as powerful for gender outcomes: where managers hold accountability for gender outcomes, there are greater numbers of women in senior roles.

The day-to-day interaction between managers and their staff provides fertile ground for enabling the talents of women to be fully realized or alternatively to be held back.

Formal accountability for gender equity can minimize the impacts of conscious and unconscious beliefs in manager behaviour and enable the playing field to be levelled.

28

EEONA's 2010 survey identified that 48% of organizations reported that they held managers accountable for diversity performance, an increase from 2008 (30%), but a decrease from 2005 (72%).

Manager accountability increases the number of women in senior roles.

The University of Melbourne's diversity policy highlights manager accountability systems, including operational review processes and setting and monitoring key performance indicators for senior staff. Freehills sets KPIs for gender diversity for staff in key management positions.

High performing gender diversity organizations have high levels of employee engagement demonstrating a clear alignment from the top cascaded down through managerial levels to all employees and accountability mechanisms mirror this.

To do

✓ Cascade accountabilities into **meaningful expectations** that managers can fulfill.

✓ Assign responsibility for developing manager KPIs and incorporating them in the **performance management system**.

A Menu of Key Performance Indicators

For managers

- Overall **gender equity** performance (representation of women in their team)
- **Equality of remuneration** for women and men in their team
- Equality of **access to development** and special assignments in the team

For senior leadership, as for managers, plus:

- **Sponsorship** of women – and their progress rate
- Inclusion of women in their **networks**
- Rewards/remuneration linked to gender diversity KPIs, including part of bonus allocated
- Promotion opportunities contingent on success
- **Reporting mechanisms** for managers who fail to promote a targeted percentage of women
- Engagement and gender surveys to report on **level of support provided** by manager for individualised working arrangements and support for career advancement after leave

---

2.5.2   Manager accountability linked to reward

One of the most powerful ways in which an organization can shape performance is through a direct link with pay. Whatever the existing practices, if manager accountability for gender balance is linked to reward, appropriate behaviour is more likely to follow. Only 8% of participants in one study felt that their company had successfully linked gender parity goals with compensation and incentives.

To overcome manager bias, one firm made pay dependent on managers' effectiveness at performance ratings, and also required them to communicate their ratings and feedback to subordinates. ING linked part of each business unit's bonus pool to the achievement of specific diversity goals.

At Chubb Corporation, those managers who supported the greatest levels of advancement coupled with the best results for the year were rewarded with large bonuses for re-investment in diversity-related programs.

Goldman Sachs in 2010 announced the introduction of a new diversity scorecard through which senior managers' bonus payments will be linked to their success in encouraging and implementing diversity. Their 50 top managers are assessed on their participation in activities designed to increase diversity, their support for diversity, and the diversity of people recruited into their teams. Their purpose is for measurement to drive home the diversity message.

To do

✓   Ensure there is a **link** between managers' achievements and the recognition and reward system with formal recognition for managers who meet their expectations. Are there consequences for failing to meet expectations?

✓   Ensure **appropriate checks and balances** in the recognition and reward system so that it is held in high regard in the organization.

2.5.3   Managers equipped and trained for success

Given that gender bias is often unconscious and unintended, managers need to be supported with constructive learning and development opportunities to create awareness and build skills so that they can enact their accountabilities.

Opening managers up to the unintended consequences of their actions can be a powerful motivating force for change. Just over half the Australian firms interviewed by Nesbit and Seeger reported that diversity and gender training was a part of their efforts to increase gender representation, whereas only 14% of participants in a Bain survey identified they had received gender parity training.

Diversity training can lead to decreased prejudice and lowering of implicit stereotypes and so is an important component in any change program. Training supports behaviour change: stereotypes about women as managers have been shifting. Male man agers characterise women as more agentic and confident, and rate women as more leader-like than they did 15 years ago, however, they still tend to see women as possessing fewer of the characteristics of successful managers than men. On the other hand, female managers now view women as more like successful managers than men, reversing their assumptions from 15 years ago.

> *"We need to make leadership appointments, not technical ones. It will require focus, but it's absolutely the right thing to do for the business. Our culture and performance will be all the better for it."*
> Grant O'Brien, CEO, Woolworths

Key manager training at Freehills includes improving career conversations, and challenging mindsets and assumptions about gender. IBM Canada has engaged over 3,000 managers in diversity training that is designed to assist them to leverage differences and to be able to lead with a full appreciation of how inclusion benefits business. This training is complemented by a booklet that gives managers strategies for having dialogues with their staff, identifying their needs and setting goals for the manager and employee relationship.

Tailored learning programs that assist managers to surface their own assumptions, consider new ways of operating, and identify the benefits to be gained, support managers to achieve their accountabilities and responsibilities.

> **To do**
>
> ✓ Identify and **support manager learning** needs.
>
> ✓ Provide managers with training and coaching to increase their awareness of the impact of **managerial behaviour** on diverse talent, and how to develop a more flexible listening and working style.

Checklist of Leadership visibility and direction actions

Identify the extent to which your organization has implemented the actions, using the rating system:

1. We already do this well
2. In train, with room for improvement
3. We don't do this, or do it poorly

Leadership visibility and direction actions	Rating
2.1 Purpose	
• Identify and communicate the business advantages that accrue from a better gender representation in your organisation. • Having identified the benefits, create a brief narrative that can help senior leaders articulate the purpose to others. • Integrate the business benefits into the organisation's overall strategy. The framework in 2.1 can be used to help identify the specific business advantages for your organisation.	
2.2 Demonstrating commitment	
2.2.1 CEO modelling • Supply the CEO with data on the business case, advocate for change and challenge decisions that may be biased. • Provide gender coaching for the CEO to support his/her leadership.	

Leadership visibility and direction actions	Rating
2.2.2 Gender balanced senior executive group • Identify or shape the strategy to increase the representation of women at the top. • Become involved in selection processes for senior positions: ensure that HR staff or recruitment consultants are briefed to provide a gender-balanced shortlist, and hold them to account. Ensure that selection processes are transparent and considered. • Provide group or individual coaching for senior women to support them in promoting and maintaining their visibility, dealing with the dilemmas and challenges of being highly visible role models and forging new ground. • Provide coaching for the CEO and senior male executives in managing a more gender-neutral engagement with their colleagues. • Work with the Executive Committee to identify key drivers of the culture with an emphasis on managing backlash, risks of transformation and recognition of success.	
2.2.3 Senior executive role models and champions • Create awareness of the need for role models, identify them and recognise their actions. • Advocate for change, assess your own behaviour and become a role model. If you don't know how, get training, advice, support and coaching from someone who does. • Create a positive narrative that provides a vision of gender fairness within the context of what the business needs/wants to achieve, reinforce business benefits. • Reinforce the importance of leadership by the CEO and Exco and what can be expected from them (specify public actions that will be observable).	
2.2.4 Sustaining commitment • Keep the issue on the agenda. • Encourage the organisation to see gender diversity strategies and programs as long term commitments, not just this year's fad. • Embed the gender diversity strategy and programs in the overall business strategy and programs. • Make sure progress is noticed and celebrated.	

Leadership visibility and direction actions	Rating
2.3 Strategic focus	
2.3.1 Embedded strategy • Connect diversity purpose and business case into the strategy. • Create a dashboard/scorecard to make targets more meaningful and integrated, then assign resources, work out how they can be a part of the overall business scorecard and therefore linked explicitly to business outcomes.	
2.3.2 Integrated policy • Identify key principles or objectives to guide policy development or review. • Audit other organisational policies so that they support and align with the diversity policy to avoid inconsistencies. • Communicate the policy throughout the organisation. • Ensure the policy is linked to your culture change program.	
2.3.3 Meaningful targets • Review and advocate for specific targets that will help drive gender diversity implementation. • Ensure they are clearly defined, strategically oriented and readily measured.	
2.4 Progress	
• Create or support visible accountability mechanisms such as a senior level diversity council, external advisory group comprising high profile membership, CEO bulletins, annual diversity report (public), diversity dashboards that assign clear expectations and responsibilities to organisational leadership, managers and individuals, and success stories of managers and women. • Provide a gender diversity reporting mechanism that identifies blockages in the system.	

Leadership visibility and direction actions	Rating
2.5 Accountability	
2.5.1 Aligned accountability • Cascade accountabilities into meaningful expectations that managers can fulfil. • Assign responsibility for developing manager KPIs and incorporating them into the performance management system.	
2.5.2 Accountability linked to reward • Ensure there is a link between managers' achievements and the recognition and reward system with formal recognition for managers who meet their expectations. Are there consequences for failing to meet expectations? • Ensure appropriate checks and balances in the recognition and reward system so that it is held in high regard in the organisation.	
2.5.3 Managers equipped and trained for success • Identify and support manager learning needs. • Provide managers with training and coaching to increase their awareness of the impact of managerial behaviour on diverse talent, and how to develop a more flexible listening and working style.	

What are three key actions that would help progress Leadership visibility and direction in your organisation?

1. _____

2. _____

3. _____

3.

BUILDING AN INCLUSIVE CULTURE

"It seems to me that we can be doing more than programs. In many cases, we have to change the rules. The rules have been invented by men for men."
~ Gordon Cairns, Chair and Non-Executive Director

Culture sets the tone for behaviour in organizations. Organizational cultures reflect the values, attitudes and behaviours of those in dominant roles. For women and other minority groups to be accepted into leadership roles requires new ways of thinking about leadership and new leadership behaviours, which entails cultural change.

3.1 DIVERSE PERSPECTIVES

Review 3.1: Does your organization's culture encourage the expression of multiple perspectives?

✔✔✔	My organization's culture enables the open expression of diverse perspectives
✔✔	My organization promotes inclusive practices, although that doesn't always translate into action
✔	Despite the rhetoric, the expression of minority perspectives is not widely valued
✗	It is necessary to do as the dominant culture does if you want to fit in

3.1.1 Inclusive culture

Many top organizations espouse diversity as an organizational value, yet many practices designed to increase diversity, such as flexible work arrangements, actually do little to support women's inclusion. Instead, they create a context in which women's needs are separated out as different, while the dominant masculine culture remains the same.

In a UK-based study, informal practices constrained the way in which women could use the diversity provisions that were available. Management acknowledged the organization's masculine norms and values, but there was little attempt to surface and challenge the powerful informal practices that reinforced them.

Organizational culture and everyday work experience strongly correlated with workplace engagement in a European study of more than 8,000 workers and corporate culture was seen as the most significant barrier to women's career development in a second European study.

Organizational environments are dominated by masculine values, norms and ways of operating. This is nowhere more evident than in the higher leadership echelons, where leadership is associated with competitiveness, confidence, decisiveness and individualism. In particular, descriptions and evaluations of male and female leadership style and capabilities vary enormously. A man's gender is a seamless fit to the executive suite and it is the norm. A woman's gender on the other hand interferes with perceptions of her legitimacy to hold positions of leadership authority.

"We've been focused on building a strong inclusive culture for many years now to ensure that we can attract and motivate the best talent possible, regardless of gender, ethnicity, religion or sexual preference. As part of this, we know that to improve the representation of women in senior leadership roles we need unwavering commitment. This requires the courage to try new things and challenge long held mindsets and unconscious bias."
Ian Narev, CEO, CBA

In organizations with few senior women, expectations about behaviour and style are firmly male. 'Women take care and men take charge'. Women are judged by the same standards, and face a significant double bind: if women demonstrate typically female attributes such as being warm, selfless, caring and friendly, they are seen as lacking competence, and therefore lose respect as leaders. However, if women project typically masculine attributes, such as being assertive, decisive, self-promoting and strong, they are criticized and not liked. Where women demonstrate more extreme male behaviours, such as aggression and autocracy, their leadership is strongly resisted.

Senior women report the need to compromise themselves, which doesn't just limit their performance, but it also undermines their sense of themselves and their ability to be authentic. An extensive review of research in this area found that women are most successful where they can balance out double binds by combining assertive, task focused and decisive behaviour with kindness, helpfulness to others and warmth.

Women need to appear to be both competent and warm, that is, male and female, to be both respected and liked in senior roles.

The good news is that where there are more than token numbers of women, there is greater latitude in gender roles. Women experience a greater sense of acceptance, higher satisfaction with the organization and greater optimism about their career.

Not all men feel able to express themselves freely; not all men live up to the picture of the male manager and not all are equally ambitious. Broadening the range of styles expressed in the organization provides similar flexibility to men as well as women.

In the US, Harley Davidson commenced a program designed to empower all employees, enabling them to contribute using their own voice. Organizational decision-making structures were flattened, creating a consensus-based model that enabled all employees, regardless of gender or race, to be true partners in the business. There was a strong drive to change culture, creating inclusion, openness, equality, the opportunity for everyone to demonstrate their own unique talents and to be recognized. The program commenced in the mid 1990s and Harley Davidson attributes its subsequent business success to it.

An organization will have overcome the impediments to better representation of women where both men and women feel encouraged by the culture to openly express themselves, and where role prescriptions are broadened to accept the range of differences that people bring.

In addition, women's talent and ambition may be suppressed as they adjust their expectations of what they might personally achieve. Women (and men) don't see evidence of women holding senior positions, which impacts their assessment of whether women are suitable for such roles. As a consequence, women's self-efficacy about their leadership abilities and expectations reduces, as they avoid setting themselves up for failure.

Women who do succeed tend to have an extraordinary level of capability. This in turn contributes to further unfairness, as the measuring stick for women to be successful is set unrealistically high.

Women must have extraordinary capability to be seen as having equal influence to men and yet are also expected to be responsible for changing their own circumstances. Women do not have sufficient power and influence to make the changes required; they do not have the power and influence to change strategy, culture and systems without men's engagement.

"What really matters is changing underlying mindsets and behaviours. We've come a long way in our journey towards a customer service culture. I believe that diversity is a big part of the next stage in our cultural journey."
Ralph Norris, former CEO, CBA

People are more resistant to women's influence than to men's, for example, when women speak up to defend their turf, they are labelled 'control freaks' whereas men are labelled 'passionate'. Disagreeing can get women into trouble; men get away with disagreeing much more often than women do, again limiting women's influence.

Women tend to say 'I'm sorry' or to apologize much more often than men. For women, this is a technique to establish rapport and build relationship whereas for men apologies tend to be seen as reducing status. Men are less likely to admit fault if they don't need to, again, as this has status implications. Women are also more likely to seek advice than men and to be indirect when telling others what to do. This is an important part of the prevailing power dynamic in senior organizational echelons.

Women may be seen as unable to project the appropriate authority for senior roles, seen from a male perspective. They are granted less power and influence when they are judged without understanding that this is a difference of style rather than capability. Senior women also identify that they more often need to influence others without formal authority.

A study that tracked how women executives were perceived at three time points over 40 years in the United States has shown a significant increase in positive perceptions. A summary of the findings appears in Figure 1.

Where organizations promote and develop a profile of leadership that integrates characteristics generally associated with women, women will experience a sound leadership capabilities fit. Opening up the range of leadership styles benefits women, men and organisations.

Figure 1. Change in perceptions of women as executives

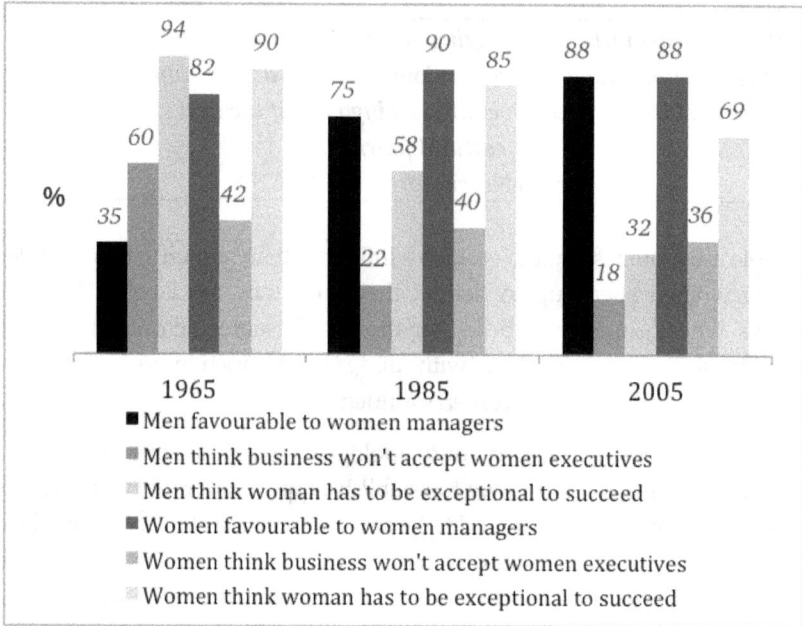

	1965	1985	2005

- ■ Men favourable to women managers
- ▦ Men think business won't accept women executives
- ▨ Men think woman has to be exceptional to succeed
- ■ Women favourable to women managers
- ▦ Women think business won't accept women executives
- ▨ Women think woman has to be exceptional to succeed

To do

✓ **Conduct a cultural audit** that provides data on acceptance of diversity.

✓ Build **leadership models** that encourage and support diverse styles.

✓ **Conduct dialogue workshops** that provide a supportive atmosphere for surfacing, exploring and questioning the gender beliefs that govern practices and assist in **identifying behaviours that support an inclusive culture.**

3.2 MYTHS CHALLENGED

There are many myths that surround women's suitability for leadership roles in organizations. Understanding the evidence base can help to counter myths and open up progress.

The following eight myths are commonly held.

MYTH 1: *It's just a matter of time before the talent pipeline filters enough women into senior roles*

The most effective strategy for increasing representation of women at senior levels is appointing women to boards and senior executive teams. Where women's presence at senior levels is normalized rather than tokenistic, there is an increased number of senior women, more women in management roles and more women are top earners. Research on US companies has shown that increases in female board members contributes to increases in female senior executives.

In most professions, there have been at least 50% female graduates for two decades, indicating that supply is not the issue but instead that barriers to progress exist within organizations.

Female graduates in Australian organizations begin their work with smaller roles and lower salaries (averaging $A3,000), receive fewer developmental assignments, are less likely to be placed in line management roles and are less likely to have sponsors. The pipeline is not a fair, failsafe way to identify and develop female talent.

MYTH 2: *Quotas are the only way to get change/quotas undermine meritocracy*

There are strong views regarding legislated quotas for women in leadership roles. Some believe that quotas are the only way that change will occur while others believe that quotas undermine meritocracy and will do more harm than good.

There is no evidence that women hired as a result of quota systems are less competent. In Norway, where quotas for board representation were introduced and achieved, there is no reported evidence of a lack of competence and no detrimental impacts on organizational performance.

There is however evidence that organizations are not particularly meritocratic.

Numerous biases constrain women's development and selection for senior roles. Women are discriminated against even where they have identical capabilities and performance as men.

Unfortunately, a widespread belief that women chosen to meet quotas are less competent may prime some women to believe they are less competent and therefore will have a damaging effect on women's self-efficacy, performance, and interest in leadership roles.

Taking a longer-term perspective, there is evidence that quotas have increased the representation of women and changed attitudes to female leadership. While strong opposition was experienced in the first generation of quota-driven change, over succeeding generations there have been positive outcomes. In local councils in India, for example, quotas have contributed to an increased representation of women in elected roles, higher leadership ambitions and aspirations for girls, gaps in educational achievement have decreased, parents' aspirations for their daughters have increased and the exposure to female leadership has improved men's perceptions of women's leadership capability.

MYTH 3: Women who make it to the top are more masculine than the men

---

When women are present in token numbers, we're primed to see them, and to judge their actions, as women. And we talk about them as women, not as leaders or bosses. We don't think of male leaders as men but as leaders.

As a personal survival mechanism, in circumstances where women are made to feel inferior, some women cast aside what it means to be a woman, become as 'unwomanly' as possible and become hostile to other women.

They become part of the dominant group (men), sometimes take on dominant group member characteristics, and behave in the same way to exclude members of the non-dominant group.

This is often referred to as the "Queen Bee" syndrome. Queen Bees hold on to their power as the token woman by denigrating other women as 'emotional', expressing anti-female attitudes, and avoiding female-focused programs and gatherings. Such women who perform well in male gender-stereotyped roles are not liked. They attract negative reactions that focus primarily on their interpersonal capabilities. Both women and men see them as less desirable as bosses, compared with men described in similar ways.

Paradoxically, this personal survival strategy, which typically appears under scarcity conditions, serves to justify the status quo: it reduces positive role modelling and reinforces bias against women in senior, non-traditional roles.

These circumstances also undermine women's willingness to tackle inequality, and reduce their interest in collective action.

MYTH 4: There aren't more women in senior roles because there aren't enough women with the right capabilities

---

Is there a female talent scarcity? Do women not have what it takes? Recruiters and search firms claim it can be difficult identifying female candidates for senior roles and the responding tactic many organizations have taken is to require at least one woman on the short list.

Here's some contrary evidence – in a European study of more than 20,000 managers, women were rated more highly on 8 out of 10 leadership characteristics. In a significant review of 45 studies of transformational leadership, females were rated as significantly more capable than men. There's no shortage of this kind of evidence – women do have the behavioural leadership capabilities it takes for top jobs.

There may however be an experience gap for some women – because women are much less likely to receive high profile assignments and line management opportunities, which are a conduit to the C-suite, some may lack key experiences important for senior roles.

Another factor at play is what's called "shifting hiring criteria", which means that gender biases shift the requirements for roles depending on whether women display behaviour judged stereotypically female or male. When women are seen as competent (male) but not warm (female), hiring criteria shifts away from a primary importance on competence to an increased importance on social skills, and women are then seen as lacking and so are not selected for the role. When women are perceived as competent but 'cold' they experience the double disadvantage of having their high competence dismissed and their lower social skills over-emphasized. Men with the same lower level of social skills are not disadvantaged in this way. Women who are competent may not be judged so by those involved in hiring decisions.

MYTH 5: Men are the ones who have to change

Unconscious assumptions about gender are shared by men and women.

Despite the evidence regarding women's leadership capabilities, both men and women are equally as likely to unconsciously believe that men's characteristics match those required for leadership while women's are associated with support roles.

Women and men are as likely to express gender stereotypes and perceive women as empathic and warm, and men as strong and ambitious. Women are as likely as men to favour male leaders over female leaders.

For significant change to occur, both men and women need to address their unconscious beliefs and become aware of how they may bias behaviour. There's more on unconscious assumptions, what they are and how they work in the next section 3.3 Bias acknowledged.

MYTH 6: *Once one woman has made it, it's easy for the rest to follow*

Both women and men believe that as long as one woman has made it, any woman can make it to the C-suite. The existence of a token woman or women, that is 15% or fewer, creates a belief that the glass ceiling has been breached and mobility for women into top roles is now possible. The evidence, however, suggests that once a small number of women have made it to the top, similar progress for other women stalls.

This seems to be based on a belief that if one woman has made it, everything has been done that needs to be done, and any woman can make it to the top. Safeguards such as monitoring selection practices, for example, are no longer seen as necessary.

Once there's a token woman at the top, women believe their organization is fair, and their commitment to the organization is reinforced. Even where token conditions don't change over time, women continue to believe that hiring is fair. As long as there's a minimum 10% senior female leadership, men also view hiring practices as fair, feel comfortable being in the majority and believe their majority is legitimate.

Highly visible token women and token hiring practices can undermine women's willingness to tackle inequality and particularly undermine their interest in collective action.

Shifting women's representation from 10% to 30% or more is relatively difficult, and is unlikely to happen without explicit intervention.

MYTH 7: *Women don't have the same natural ambition as men*

There's no specific evidence that shows that men and women do or do not have the same amounts of ambition, but there is plentiful research that shows why it is difficult and complex for women to openly express ambition.

In organizations, a woman's talent and ambitions may be suppressed where there are no women holding senior positions; the lack of female presence sends the message that women are not suitable for such roles. Women's self-efficacy about their leadership abilities and expectations reduce, along with their ambitions, and becomes a strategy for avoiding failure. In such environments, men similarly learn that women are "not suitable" for leadership and lack ambition. A negative cycle is subsequently created where low numbers of women at the top is taken as evidence that women do not have the desire or the ability to succeed.

At the personal level, in situations where gender is "primed" (made salient), behaviour is more closely attuned to stereotypes. For example, in situations requiring performance on a task that has a negative stereotype associated with it, e.g., women are bad at maths, stereotype threat, the fear of being judged and treated unfairly, can come into play. Stereotype threat results in reduced performance on the task compared with circumstances when gender is not primed or where the stereotype is countered by making different criteria salient. Where women are primed to see themselves as particularly bright and capable their performance is at least as good on maths tasks as men.

Women respond to subtle cues such as "women are bad at maths" and "I am a woman", by unconsciously lowering their performance expectations, while their performance anxiety increases. Attempts to counteract these messages involve significant mental resources, which are then not available to the task at hand. This effect has its greatest impact for those women who have greater concern for their status, who care the most about their maths skills and how well they do on tests: their greater anxiety reduces the mental resources available for the task.

Stereotype threat does more than increase anxiety and decrease performance, it can also lead women to limit the choices they make about career options that require them to join male-dominated environments. Women have a tendency to avoid situations that are male-dominated, as they don't see themselves fitting in. The need to fit and to belong is a fundamental psychological need and one that impacts significantly on women's choice of career, their interest in promotion, and their ability to project themselves into the most senior level leadership roles.

Visible role modelling of women in authority is associated with an increase in women's ambitions as women are better able to identify with success.

MYTH 8: Women need to improve their confidence and speak up

Gender schema prescribes different communication styles and approaches as appropriate for men and women. In organizations, men's linguistic style is the norm, and women's patterns can make them appear less competent and self-assured than they may be.

Women's stereotypical communication style is relationship oriented and status differences are minimized, while men's is power oriented and focused on increasing status differences. Women tend to downplay their certainty, and men are more likely to minimize their doubts. This can be interpreted as a lack of confidence in women, whereas it may instead reflect a desire to be modest and avoid boasting. Men are also less likely than women to ask questions believing that this loses face by admitting to uncertainty. They may therefore judge women, who are more likely to ask questions, as lacking knowledge. Women prefer to share credit, by using 'we' while men use 'I'.

Women tend to minimize their own contribution, compared with men. Men are much more likely to self-promote and to confidently and assertively state their achievements and capabilities, whether or not they are accurate.

These style differences are not engrained, and show up in shared male and female interactions: in female only interactions, women openly seek power and compete with each other.

Women's contributions and capabilities may be overlooked due to their different communication style.

Many women believe that if they simply do a good job, their superior performance will be recognized and they will achieve success.

However, because of style and expectation differences between men and women and dominant male norms, women's performance and capabilities may be neither seen nor heard. In one organisation, women reported that the messages they were trying to give about their career commitment did not seem to be recognised by their managers unless they made them particularly forcibly.

Women's style differences are often attributed to a lack of confidence and women are exhorted to be more confident and to speak up. Simply expecting women to learn how to take credit for example, may backfire, as many women believe that they won't be liked if they do so: research evidence shows this to be well-founded.

Managers who are aware of and publicly acknowledge different communication styles, and responsively adapt their own style, increase the opportunity for women's full voice to be heard and full range of talents to be used.

To do

✓ **Be aware** that there are many myths surrounding gender and roles and that these can impede women's progress.

✓ **Surface assumptions** and myths and promote dialogue about what's possible

✓ Promote dialogue that enables **multiple perspectives** to be expressed and debated.

3.3 BIAS ACKNOWLEDGED

There is an increasing awareness that unconscious gender beliefs impacts decisions relating to men and women in organizations and that this is an important area for change, but less is known about what unconscious bias actually is, how it works and what it takes to change it.

Bias is unfair, illegitimate or unjustifiable judgment that goes beyond the objective needs or evidence in a particular situation.

Unconscious bias is an umbrella term that is used to cover a range of different social, psychological and cultural factors and influences that all have a part to play in developing and maintaining our world-views including our gender schema, but of which we are unaware.

As humans, we have many unconscious beliefs and biases that affect our leadership decision-making. Biases like confirmation bias, which leads managers to ignore evidence that doesn't fit their views, or loss aversion, that makes them too cautious, lead to sub-optimal business decisions. Having these biases is simply a normal part of the human condition, and not an indication of ill intention.

Gender schema is a fundamental part of our conscious and unconscious belief systems, and it may bias our interpretations and decisions.

"Two things are critical to making a step change–having aligned leadership that genuinely believes in the business benefits, and surfacing and systematically eliminating the hidden biases that are a very real part of most organizations."
David Peever, Former CEO, Rio Tinto

Gender biases lead managers to view talent in pre-determined ways, which leads to inequities and a loss of current and future capability and commitment. Bias based on gender plays out in three main domains: the person, the group and society. At the personal level it impacts expectations and behaviours of ourselves and others as men and women.

At the level of the group, bias favours dominant group members, men, over non-dominant group members, women. At the level of society, gender biases drive culturally held power disparities between men and women.

Bias against women may be consciously held and openly expressed. However, most people are aware that the open expression of bias against women is not always socially acceptable. What they are less aware of is the impact of unconscious bias, which affects decisions without awareness. Even more challenging is that both women and men can demonstrate the same unconscious bias against women in leadership, and even those who openly express egalitarian attitudes can demonstrate the same unconscious bias. On the plus side, having unconscious beliefs doesn't necessarily lead to discrimination.

3.3.1 Gender schema

Gender is a concept that we learn early and thoroughly, and it is a primary guide for negotiating our actions in the world. Most importantly, it is a fundamental concept in understanding who we are, in the development of our sense of identity.

The most common question to follow a woman's announcement that she is pregnant is "is it a boy or a girl?" From birth, we engage in the world with gender schema as an important guide, and this shapes, enables and constrains us in particular ways.

As our gender schema is learnt so early and so thoroughly, it becomes unconscious to the point that, if we reflect on it at all, it seems the natural order of things.

Men are typically associated with a set of traits labeled 'agentic', while women are typically associated with a set of traits labeled 'communal'.

Our gender schema ascribes and prescribes certain traits as male and others as female. These sets of traits form a schema, or stereotype, about what men and women are like, and should be like, an is set out in the table below.

Gender schema is well researched in more than 25 nations. Individuals may have their own personal stereotypes, reflecting their own set of beliefs, and yet people recognize the culturally accepted gender schema, giving it a high degree of consensus and credibility.

Our gender schema guides how we perceive men and women and how we judge their actions. It guides the way we interact with men and with women. This is both advantageous and disadvantageous. It helps us to navigate highly complex situations and processes with greater ease and simplicity. But it also constrains the way we interact with individuals, because we apply group characteristics regardless of whether or not they apply to the particular individual. We tend to disregard information that doesn't confirm our gender schema, seeing it as a situational factor rather than something relevant to the individual.

Female: Communal traits	Male: Agentic traits
– Focus on the needs of others	– Focus on own needs
– Empathy	– Task oriented
– Understanding	– Tough
– Gentle	– Competitive
– Kind	– Assertive
– Soft	– Competent
– Expressive	– Ambitious
– Fearful	– Bad but bold
– Wonderful	– Adventurous
– Weak	– Dominant
– Sentimental	– Forceful
– Submissive	– Independent

Both female and male sets of traits are desirable, but in different ways. Men, as agentic, are respected, while women, as communal, are liked, reinforcing differential power attributions. Male traits are associated with power therefore with authority and status while female traits are associated with nurturing, lower status, and support positions.

Interestingly, both men and women have more positive implicit beliefs about women than about men. Women's caregiving appears to explain why men and women share this view. Men on the other hand are associated with the threat of danger and violence and so implicit beliefs about men tend to be more negative.

For most people, these associations are 'common sense'. They are such well learned associations that we don't have to think hard to match the traits with the 'right' gender.

These associations become stereotypes: we expect men and women to behave in these ways and this is the basis of prejudice which is an individual-level attitude (whether subjectively positive or negative) toward groups and their members, that creates or maintains hierarchical status relations between groups.

There are distinct subtypes of gender beliefs: Hostile and Benevolent, with each applying to both men and women. Hostile Sexism is based on a negative reaction to power differences and to women's increasing attempts to reduce the power differential. Benevolent Sexism is based on complementary interdependence where the stereotypical virtues of each gender are extolled.

Hostile Sexism towards women is characterized by negativity towards women who do not behave in accordance with strict gender stereotypes. Those with Hostile attitudes believe women want to gain power by having control over men, they deny discrimination at work, consider that feminists make unreasonable demands and see women as sexual teasers.

Benevolent Sexism towards women sees men's and women's roles as distinctly different and complementary, that men are incomplete without women. Men who express Benevolent Sexism towards women believe that women should be cherished and protected, that women have a purity and a superior morality to men's and that men should sacrifice their wellbeing to provide for the women in their lives.

Hostility towards men suggests that men always fight to get control, most men engage in sexual harassment and seek to have power over women, men want traditional relationships with their wife looking after the house and children, and men are child-like including acting like babies when they're sick.

Finally, Benevolence towards men sees men as useful for providing financial security and that every woman should have a male partner who will cherish her; she won't be fulfilled without a long term relationship with a man. Men are more willing to take risks and put themselves in danger to protect others. Even if a woman works, she should also look after her man at home.

These different forms of sexism underscore the ambiguity in this domain and the subtlety of some of the distinctions. A man expressing Benevolent Sexism towards a woman may feel genuine affection and seek to be helpful, without either the woman or the man understanding how patronizing the behaviour may be.

Benevolent Sexism is a particular problem in the search for equality: individuals who endorse it usually also endorse Hostile Sexism and other attitudes that support gender inequality. Benevolent Sexism actively undermines women's attempts at equality because it seems 'nice'.

Hostile and Benevolent Sexism are complementary and together justify the existence of gender stereotypes, making them seem completely natural: Hostile Sexism expresses hostility to women who behave outside of accepted stereotypes while Benevolent Sexism rewards those women who fulfill them. Such a pattern sees men as wise benefactors rather than hostile suppressors, and is particularly effective. It fosters loyalty and affection between the dominant and non-dominant groups. Paradoxically, it serves to reinforce the status differences between the genders, with an effective system of benevolence as the carrot and hostility as the stick.

Benevolent Sexism undermines women's resistance to inequality. Women who tend to accept Benevolent Sexism are opposed to attempts to create equality, to feminists and are prepared to trade-off their subordination to men for their protection and benevolence.

3.3.2 Gender schema and leadership
Women in male dominated firms perceive greater psychological and behavioural differences between men and women, and tend to evaluate women's attributes less favourably than women in organizations with a greater representation of women.

Women are more likely to be found at higher levels in non-manufacturing organizations where there are relatively more women at lower management levels, there is higher management turnover and salaries are lower, reinforcing that cultural assumptions rather than capability are key reasons for a lack of women.

Females spend more time establishing their credibility and finding their niche in order to be noticed, while men spend their time mastering particular business competencies which gives them added advantage in demonstrating their skill.

Additionally, where women behave in ways that are out of keeping with gender stereotypes, they can be punished by social rejection and become the personal target of negative judgments: this can lead to negative career impacts. Research shows that where women were successful at male-dominated jobs they were disliked and seen particularly unfavourably: such women were seen as less desirable as bosses. Interestingly, women perceived as successful and who behave with appropriately communal behaviour are liked. Women identified as mothers are automatically seen as communal which neutralizes negative behavioural impacts from success. While being a mother has generally been believed to be disadvantageous for women in management, it appears that it can also have positive benefits.

The cultural barriers to greater representation of women are held as much by women as by men; culture and belief is not just about men and it is not just men who must change.

Men who have a strong sense of fair play are more aware of gender bias. These men are more highly attuned to issues of fairness, and a lack of fairness, and feel a need to redress imbalances. Men demonstrate their commitment to fair play by being willing to stand up and advocate for greater fairness for women. Ernst & Young's Cultivating men as allies program focuses men on the negative impact of gender beliefs on men and women, and what they stand to gain which helps increase their sense of fair play and engagement.

While gender schema have value in simplifying a complex world, they also suppress and limit our behavioural repertoire.

Where behavioural differences between men and women are held to be biologically predetermined, men and women tend to support gender schema and believe women have appropriate access to leadership opportunities. Men are more likely to engage in discriminatory behaviour and to feel justified in doing so. At this stage, the research examining the biological bases of behaviour has not demonstrated this link.

From birth, women's lives have been shaped by the need to think of others first, to give up their needs to men, to be agreeable and warm and friendly. From birth, men's lives are shaped by the expectation that their needs come first, that they set the direction and agenda and that they should be in charge. In organizations, gender schema guides us as to what's acceptable and what's not in a leader, and that's typically male.

When men 'act like women' their status falls and their gender and sexual identity are questioned, whereas when women 'act like men' their status rises but their femininity and social attractiveness are questioned.

Notwithstanding more recent discussion about the suitability of women's typical relational, communal style for leadership roles, the decisions about who gets to lead continue to be filtered through a male lens. The pervasiveness of unconscious gender schema means that decisions about legitimate leadership are routinely biased against women and in favour of men. Women face the dilemma of being damned for being competent as leaders, or doomed for being 'proper' warm women.

Gender schema operates both consciously and unconsciously. Some people fully and openly endorse the differences between men and women, see them as biologically determined and believe them to be immutable. Others endorse a view that men and women are not different at all; that they can be and do anything. Some who consciously endorse the latter view are quite unaware that they unconsciously hold the former view and that it impacts on their decisions. The following section helps understand more about bias and how gender schema can both consciously and/or unconsciously bias our behaviour.

Our gender schema is a belief system rather than a fact system. For example, when men and women are given a financial incentive to do well on an empathy task, men and women perform equally well, and when women are primed to 'think like a man', their emotional sensitivity decreases to be the same as men's. And where men see great social value resulting from expressions of empathy, their emotional sensitivity is on a par with women's.

When we don't think of ourselves as 'male' or 'female', our judgments are more similar than different. The key focus of our shared gender schema is on difference between the genders, despite significant research demonstrating that there is far greater similarity than difference. Research shows remarkable similarity between men's and women's psychological traits, such as self-esteem and cognitive ability; the few areas of difference relate to physical strength, and attitudes towards sex and aggression.

3.3.3   What is unconscious bias?

Our unconscious capacities play a significant role in our practical decision-making, ensuring that it is far from being the deliberative, systematic and analytical process we believe it to be. Thinking and judgment are already well under way before we know it. There is a wide range of heuristics and biases that we use to make sense of the world that aid our decision-making. While they are positive in helping us make sense of the world, they are also powerful contributors to misjudgment.

Our conscious minds process about 40 pieces of information each second, which is a small share of the total information available to us. It's estimated that our unconscious mind deals with between 8 million and 40 million pieces of information in that same second. Our unconscious mind handles all this information by taking a number of shortcuts using automatic associations that are learned patterns, and this significantly aids our decision-making. For example, we don't have to go into the same situation 50 times, experience it as brand new each time we do, and expend valuable conscious resources working out what to do.

Unconscious beliefs develop early in our socialization, and over time become automatic. We continue to use the same interpretations, or miss the same cues, over and over, without even knowing it. People add new beliefs as they are exposed to new experiences, cultures and attitudes. New beliefs tend to be consciously held, although it is possible for beliefs to develop without conscious awareness and simply through exposure to the social world.

Awareness that we have unconscious bias helps understand why men are disproportionately chosen ahead of women for leadership roles. It helps us understand why a rational argument, such a sound, apparently compelling business case for gender diversity isn't always enough to gain commitment to diversity programs.

3.3.4   How do unconscious beliefs impact decisions?

Our unconscious gender schema, which prescribes leadership as a male domain, lies at the heart of why men are disproportionately chosen ahead of women for leadership roles, even when managers believe they are being fair. Unconscious bias also impacts women's own choices about their careers and contributes to their avoidance of roles in male-dominated domains and careers.

Figure 2. Duality of beliefs

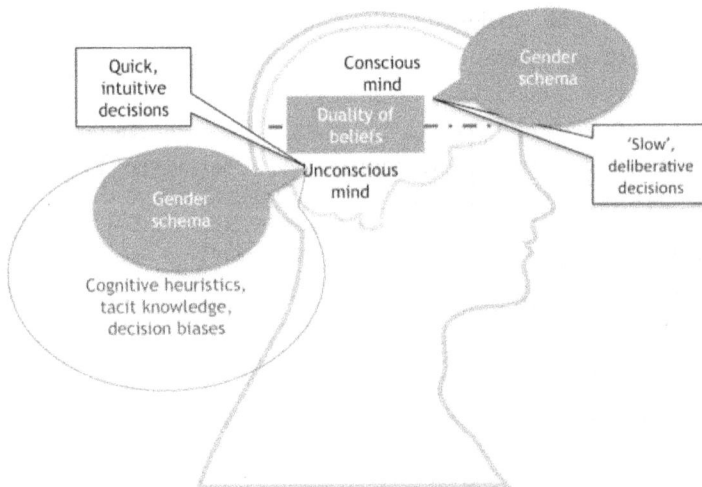

As already noted, gender schema is learnt early, thoroughly, stored in memory and accessed without awareness. What most people are unaware of is that we have an interesting duality of beliefs: our conscious and unconscious beliefs are quite likely to contradict each other. That's particularly the case for contentious issues, like gender and race. It applies to people who believe themselves to be egalitarian: conscious egalitarian beliefs co-exist with unconscious stereotypes in the same person. In general, what we say represents our conscious beliefs, while what we do, particularly our nonverbal behaviour, is more representative of our unconscious beliefs.

Unconscious beliefs influence us most when:

- We don't have clear decision criteria,
- We don't have or take the time to deliberate on our decisions,
- Information is ambiguous so it's not clear how it helps us to make the decision,
- There is no open scrutiny of the decision.

For example, in research exploring hiring decisions, the same CV was given to different 'selection committee members' and the gender of the candidate randomly assigned. When the candidate was clearly high performing or low performing, the decision was likewise very clear. However, when a candidate's qualifications for a position lay between those two extremes, the decision became more ambiguous. Under these circumstances, men were much more likely to be selected than women, despite the CVs being identical but for the name.

Conscious beliefs shape deliberative, well-considered responses where people have the opportunity to weigh the costs and benefits of various courses of action.

Unconscious beliefs influence responses that are more difficult to control, such as nonverbal responses, or responses that are automatic that people don't try to 'control'. The kinds of biases that unconscious beliefs can lead to appear in the following table.

Biased decision-making	
Affinity	Liking people most like us and favouring them over others
Expectancy	Creating expectations and interpreting others' behavior using gender schema
Confirmation	Paying attention to behaviour that confirms gender schema and disregarding that which disconfirms
Directive	Using gender schema to direct the context so that gender consistent information is elicited
Self-fulfilling prophesy	Priming behaviour based on gender, leading to gender effects, such as decreases in performance in maths tasks
Self-selection	Women's own biases cause them to opt out of opportunities
Attraction of power	Everyone wants to be in the 'in-group' so it is seen positively: out-group members are equally derogatory about the out-group

Non-dominant groups members are particularly aware of nonverbal bias. For example, managers might say the right thing, but their nonverbal behaviours undermine their words (without their awareness). People rely heavily on nonverbal behaviour to understand other people's intentions and meaning and so incongruity between verbal and nonverbal communication is noticed.

Minority group members are particularly attuned to negative behaviours of majority-group members that reveal their bias and so they are more likely to detect the incongruity and to feel dissatisfied with the interactions they have. Because they have different perspectives and rely on different information, men and women may leave conversations with fundamentally different impressions of their interactions.

Unconscious beliefs influence personal interactions and group processes and adversely impact outcomes for the non-dominant group members. Biases erode trust between group members and have a negative impact on group performance and on the performance of minority group members.

Opening managers up to this unconscious bias can be a complete revelation. Goldman Sachs divides management into four breakout groups in training– white male, white female, minorities, and non-Americans and they discuss their experience of merit. Only the white male group identified that they work in a meritocracy, being confident that hard work paid off and that promotions and salaries were fairly distributed. Members of the other three groups did not experience the organization as a meritocracy. Norton Rose provides unconscious bias training that, as Managing Partner Wayne Spanner noted, provided a 'light bulb' moment for him in understanding the impact of biases on everyday decision-making. From such an understanding, it is then key to ensure such bias does not occur.

This shows how discrimination can occur without awareness and often without intention. The basis for the decision is misattributed to a lack of skills or qualifications rather than gender.

It's important to be clear that having unconscious beliefs isn't the problem. The problem is:

• Having unconscious beliefs and not knowing you do,

• Having them and not acknowledging them, or

• Knowing you have them and not seeking to challenge them.

Acknowledging bias is particularly important. People who say they don't have unconscious beliefs make more biased hiring decisions than those who acknowledge they do.

To do
✓ Seek and **support, training and development** on unconscious associations and bias.
✓ Equip managers and team members to **understand how beliefs work,** and how they can impact on managerial decisions without awareness.
✓ Ensure there are transparent processes that include checks and balances to **guard against unconscious bias against wome**n.

3.4 BACKLASH MANAGED

A critical capability for the CEO and leadership group is to hold steady during the move to an inclusive culture, weathering resistance, backlash and unintended consequences.

"I believe that having women in leadership is important for businesses. In the past, I've worked with people who don't share my conviction. That doesn't mean I give up. I just make them accountable and push until they take action. Once they start, their conviction is bound to grow."
Kevin McCann AM, Chair & Non-Executive Director

Policies and programs to increase the representation of women are quite likely in the early stages to lead to a backlash. A range of unintended consequences can arise:

- Some organizations experience an initial drop in women in management, as women retreat to avoid scrutiny,
- A strong focus on women can disenfranchise some men, who may become vocal in their opposition to transformation initiatives and actively resist change,
- There may be performance dips in other business areas as expectations change and the focus of attention shifts,

- As pay inequities become better understood women may lobby for increases in their remuneration and their satisfaction with the organization may decrease,
- Perceived 'failures' by high profile women may become magnified and key women may be marginalized,
- The wrong kind of mentoring and support for women could paradoxically hold back their progress, or
- Managers may feel overwhelmed by the new demands of transformation; for some this may result in entrenching their prejudice.

Employees will generally deny there is unequal treatment in their organization or attribute differences to external factors that have nothing to do with the organization's actions. Being confronted with their biases can lead to resistance: backlash against change in deeply held attitudes is a normal human response.

Achievement of better gender balance tends to be seen as a women's issue, yet it is about both men and women. Without the engagement and participation of men, gender initiatives are unlikely to create the momentum desired. It is estimated that about one third of men fear a loss of status as a consequence of gender diversity programs, believing that gains for women will only come at the expense of gains for men. Where men see the introduction of gender diversity programs as a threat, their identification as men increases and they join ranks to ward off the threat. Backlash is a consequence of this. All dominant groups are liable to take such action if they feel a sense of threat.

Some men are concerned that they will make mistakes in their interactions with women and will be blamed for the challenges that women face. Other men are concerned that if they support women, they will lose face with their male colleagues. Finally, some men remain either ignorant of or unconcerned about the impact of gender assumptions.

Women too may be resistant to change, and may be particularly concerned about unwelcome visibility that they may gain as gender is discussed more openly. They may be fearful, embarrassed or hostile in response to specific programs to foster female talent. Again, this is a normal response.

When women and men act outside of stereotypes, they violate our expectations, e.g., women are supposed to be warm and communal, but they instead demonstrate the 'male' behaviours of competitiveness and drive.

In their book "The Social Psychology of Gender", Rudman and Glick provide an explanation for why backlash occurs. The research on gender shows that people are motivated to maintain self-esteem and their sense of identity in social interactions, and gender, as discussed above, is a very important part of identity. Initiatives that support women becoming senior leaders challenge our sense of identity by promoting behaviour that deviates from stereotypes.

Women themselves understand that backlash is a possibility if they behave outside of gender schema prescriptions. Fear of backlash does two things – firstly, it can prevent behaviour that deviates from prescriptions, so women stay within gender prescriptions. Secondly, having engaged in behaviour that violates gender prescriptions, women engage in recovery strategies. Recovery strategies include hiding or minimizing their 'gender-deviance': they may lie about their behaviour, hide it or engage in particularly stereotypical behaviours to win back approval. Recovery strategies both serve to reinforce stereotypes and enable people to maintain their sense of belonging to the group and with that, maintain their self-esteem.

Where women feel unsuccessful at influencing masculine work cultures they are less likely to remain within the organization. When people witness acts that violate stereotypes, they feel justified in taking punitive action, such as dislike or even harassment. For example, people can believe it is within their rights to put women in their place, which includes when they are evaluating others in hiring decisions or performance ratings. And their self-esteem improves when they do, that is, people feel better about themselves when they apply penalties for gender deviant behaviour.

Figure 3. How Backlash works

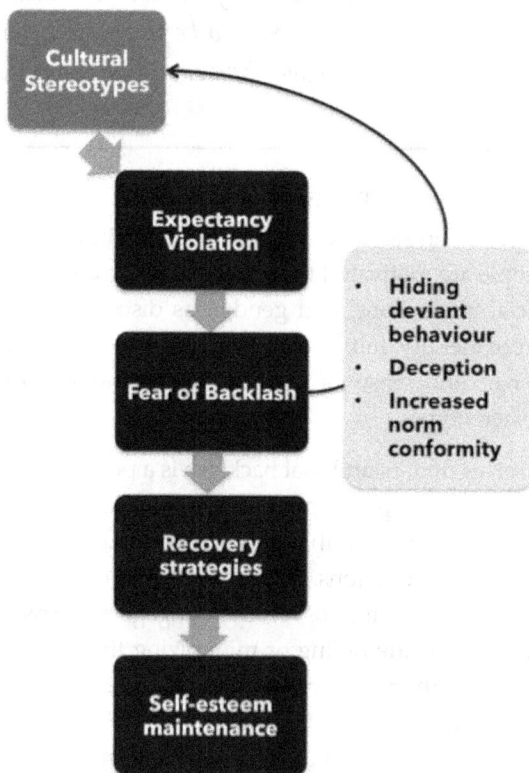

And it isn't just men who engage in backlash. Because women expend effort in reducing cognitive bias by justifying the system that treats them inequitably, they may react against other women who attempt to change the status quo. In organizations that seek to examine gender stereotypes, prejudice and discrimination, women may be part of the backlash for this reason.

Women whose behaviour lies outside of gender prescriptions, such as those in powerful positions, are most able to challenge stereotypes. However, those women are the least likely to do so if the threat of backlash is prominent. This helps understand why some high profile women are judged to be opposed to standing up for 'women's issues' or avoid identifying their gender as associated with their leadership success: they are minimizing their gender deviance to maintain their self-esteem. Unwittingly, this serves to reinforce cultural stereotypes that highlight their gender deviance.

Atypical men and women are consequently less visible and so there are fewer vanguards that challenge cultural stereotypes and fewer role models to provide a broader view of behaviour.

The fear of backlash also prevents men from appearing more 'feminine'. Research has shown that when men believe they are seen as more feminine, a common recovery strategy is to show stronger support for and engagement in physical violence, from wars to domestic violence. Another recovery strategy is to reject women who pose a threat to their male dominance, such as women who demonstrate agentic traits or who are labelled feminist.

As with all change programs, anxieties surface and some degree of resistance is likely. A softer hand is required to establish a context in which open and honest dialogue about men's and women's experiences can be conducted. It is necessary to avoid blame, and instead focus on how the organization can be improved for everyone.

To create real change requires significant cultural realignment, surfacing gender beliefs, and identifying new, shared beliefs to guide future behaviour. Opening the opportunity for dialogue can lead to moments of insight, foster mutual understanding, and provide an opportunity to surface and work with assumptions.

Awareness and careful consideration of the challenges of mindsets maximizes the true value of diversity.

Best practice organizations ensure that men, who may be resistant or concerned about gender inclusion initiatives, or indeed advocates, are involved in change processes. Where all employees are able to engage meaningfully in diversity efforts, innovative solutions and opportunities are developed. At current estimates, this kind of engagement seems to happen only about 40% of the time, so for many organizations these dialogues provide an opportunity for improving their gender diversity outcomes. Deloitte Consulting invested $8m and brought together 5,000 senior leaders in workshops that were pivotal in raising awareness of the different treatment that men and women received.

Men and women together can create new opportunities and work towards constructive change. Building in commitment to change through involvement in planning and implementation ensures that men and women both identify and share the benefits. Best practice organizations experience low levels of employee backlash and resistance as a consequence of this careful approach and are able to build momentum through their diversity initiatives.

To do

✓ Be aware that **backlash is likely** and stay attuned to its signs.

✓ Remember that backlash **can come from men and women.**

✓ **Accept all points of view** as legitimate.

✓ **Use inquiry and discussion** to help improve the overall climate and work practices for everyone.

✓ Provide **workshops, cascaded from the top,** that enable open and frank discussion about gender dynamics.

✓ Raise awareness of how **men and women think and communicate differently** about their skills and their expectations.

✓ Identify **new practices that enable genders to collaborate fairly.**

Checklist of Building an inclusive culture actions

Identify the extent to which your organization has implemented the following actions using the rating system:

1. We already do this well
2. In train, with room for improvement
3. We don't do this, or do it poorly

Building an inclusive culture	Rating
3.1 Diverse perspectives	
• Conduct a cultural audit that provides data on acceptance of diversity. • Build leadership models that encourage and support diverse styles. • Conduct dialogue workshops that provide a supportive atmosphere for surfacing, exploring and questioning the gender beliefs that govern practices assist in identifying what it means for a culture to be inclusive and behaviours that support inclusion.	
3.2 Myths Challenged	
• Be aware that there are many myths surrounding gender and roles and that these can impede women's progress. • Surface assumptions and myths and promote dialogue about what's possible. • Promote dialogue that enables multiple perspectives to be expressed and debated.	
3.3 Bias acknowledged	
• Seek and support training and development on unconscious associations and bias. • Equip managers and team members to understand how beliefs work, and how they can impact on managerial decisions without awareness. • Ensure there are transparent processes that include checks and balances to guard against unconscious bias against women.	

Building an inclusive culture	Rating
3.4 Backlash Managed	
• Be aware that backlash is likely and stay attuned to its signs. • Remember that backlash can come from men and women. • Accept all points of view as legitimate. • Use inquiry and discussion to help improve the overall climate and work practices for everyone. • Provide workshops, cascaded from the top, that enable open and frank discussion about gender dynamics. • Use them to surface powerful informal practices that reinforce masculine norms and values and raise awareness of how men and women think and communicate differently about their skills and their expectations.	

What are three key actions that would help progress Building an inclusive culture in your organisation?

1. _____

2. _____

3. _____

4.

WORK PRACTICES

"Flexibility needs to be mainstream – it's the key to unlocking a huge part of our talent pool."
~ Gail Kelly, Former CEO, The Westpac Group

Combining flexible working paths with continued career progression remains challenging, yet fundamental to achieving diversity goals and retaining talent. Increasingly, organizations are committing to a range of flexible work practices that open new opportunities to create the desired balance between work and personal commitments, and at the same time, build productivity.

4.1 DIVERSE PRACTICES SUPPORTED

Flexible work practices are fundamental to engaging women with family responsibilities. Increasingly, men are taking advantage of diverse patterns of working.

Review 4.1: Assess your organization's progress: Do you have work practices that build productivity while enabling workers to attain a preferred balance between their careers and their personal lives?

✔✔✔ People at all levels work to outcomes and objectives, working flexibly while maximizing their career progress

✔✔ People at lower levels of the organization make good use of flexible and innovative work practices and are well supported in doing so

✔ Women and other minority groups are supported to work flexibly, however, flexible working means that career progress slows

✗ Working flexibly is seen as working less and so people are reluctant to make use of the provisions because they know openly doing so will limit their career progress

Both infrastructure and managerial support are necessary to implement and support diverse working practices. Management support in aligning action with policy is a key requirement. Some managers have difficulty coping with the uncertainty of change that comes with pioneering new flexible work arrangements, and can resist such change. However, once new arrangements work out, there is often quick adoption by others.

Increased use of diverse working arrangements provides women with greater opportunity to remain in the workplace and therefore to have greater presence, which increases positive work relationships and career opportunities.

Increasingly, men want access to flexible work arrangements, and in some organizations, like Coca Cola Australia, purchasing additional annual leave that can be taken during school holiday time is increasingly popular. As managers become more accepting of flexible arrangements and both men and women model their use, they become normalized, and a part of how business is done rather than something special that needs to be done for women to fit in.

The central organizing mechanisms for work are setting clear objectives and motivating people to do their work.

Organizations such as Lenovo have instigated a management model that enables greater freedom in where and how their staff work. Rules are relaxed, office hours are more flexible and there is less centralized control over work.

Catalyst's best practice organizations offered reduced working weeks, flexible arrival and departure times, telecommuting, compressed working weeks and job sharing in their efforts to increase flexibility.

To implement a number of these practices requires practical support including availability and use of the appropriate technology and systems for flexible working, including working from home. Such innovations rely on good technological support, enabling access to the full range of tools required to get the job done. Training employees in the use of appropriate technologies and how they can be used across sites and from home helps support smarter working practices. Without such support, flexibility can be rendered meaningless.

Microsoft Australia's diversity and inclusion program is based on their core organizational values, and their diversity and inclusion strategy is overseen by a staff council: the purpose of the council is to ensure the meaningful enactment of their strategy across the total business. There is consistency between their overall vision of '…great software anytime, anywhere…' and their challenge to staff to meet their work commitments in a timeframe or schedule that suits them: their 'mantra' is 'what works for you can work for us too'.

In Catalyst's study, the organizations pursuing diverse practices experienced job engagement and commitment 10% higher than organizations not pursuing them, intention to remain in the organization was 23% higher and job satisfaction was 44% higher, indicating the power of supporting flexibility at work.

By making working hours flexible, and aligning effort to purpose and objectives, a broader diversity of talent can be engaged and retained.

4.1.1   Engagement during and following extended leave

Women's career histories contain more and longer extended leave absences than do men's. Recent research found that 26% of women versus 14% of men took an extended leave of absence. The same study found that only one third of workers thought that maternity/paternity leave programs were effective.

When women temporarily leave the workforce they experience a number of negative career consequences, including loss of income, slowed career growth, depreciation of skills and difficulty re-establishing their career.

Even for women with excellent credentials and high ambition to advance, it can be difficult to regain their career momentum.

The companies that manage women's extended leave best retain contact during the absence, have personal meetings before and after the leave, focus on reintegrating women into the workforce and monitor remuneration following return. Better companies provide advice to women on what to do when returning from leave and provide training modules during their absence.

Only 13% of Nesbit and Seeger's sample of 30 Australian organizations identified that they keep in touch with women on maternity leave. There was an industry bias, as can be seen in the following graph. Keeping the lines of communication open during leave gives women an indication that a meaningful return is possible.

As a retention strategy Mercy Health implemented a Parent's Network, sponsored by the Chief Executive Officer, and comprising a series of networking lunches for staff on parental leave. The purpose of the network was to enable staff to stay connected to each other and to the workplace while they were on leave. They also discussed parenting issues. Combined with flexible work options, the network contributes to a return rate from parental leave of 97%.

Proactive companies retain close contact with employees during extended leave, keeping them in touch with the organization and managing any skills gap that might be created during their absence.

Figure 4. Keeping in touch with women on maternity leave, by industry

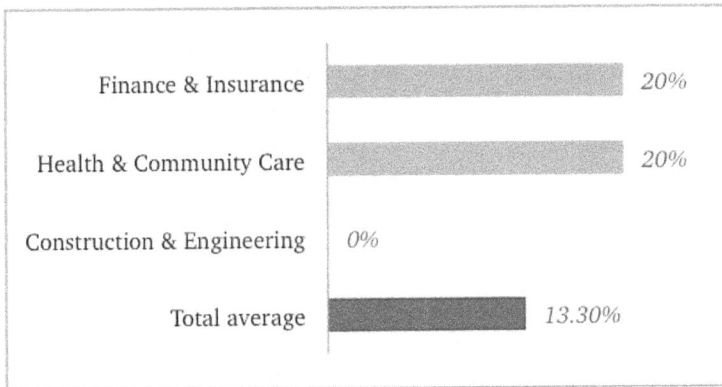

Organizations that provide structured re-engagement programs, such as tailored return to work programs or bridging programs, maximize the likelihood of successful reintegration. The ability of the manager to understand and support the needs of women returning to work is critical to their reengagement and retention. Charting a flexible re-engagement and ongoing engagement with women should not assume that their ambition is dormant or that they are happy to remain at the same level of responsibility they were at before they leave.

Sector of employment affects women's return to work following maternity leave. The community care sector reports 91% retention, finance and insurance sector 75% and construction and engineering 65% retention following maternity leave, reflecting these sectors' cultural adaptation to fit with changing female employee needs.

GM Holden Australia in the mid-2000s increased return to work from maternity leave from 67% to 92% by instituting a variety of initiatives that targeted the specific needs of women returning to work, as well as the broader cultural context. They increased flexible arrangements available, including part-time work in roles not previously available, job sharing and working from home.

Assisting women to balance family needs and responsibilities with career opportunities may continue to be important for a decade after they return.

EOWA reported a new benchmark for women's return to work following maternity leave, achieved by Shine Lawyers: 100% of women returned from maternity leave, using the available flexible working arrangements. Their Parental Support Scheme included 18 weeks paid maternity leave, an additional 20% of an employee's base salary in childcare costs until their children reach school age, and facilitation of access to childcare centres throughout the country. Two of the 30 women so far involved in the scheme were promoted into senior management roles on their return to work.

Those organizations that foster women's confidence as they return to work and shape meaningful roles whilst maintaining flexibility, and focus on capability rather than time served, will most quickly reap the benefits of full performance.

It is necessary to think beyond the first year or two following return from leave, to help women map out their future.

Organizations may or may not be aware of the full extent of career compromise they create, as women experiencing rigidity or insensitivity to family issues are more likely to quit quietly than to ask for what they need.

Flexible working arrangements can increase organizational productivity by returning women to maximum capability through re-engagement programs, by identifying the specific needs of individual women and tailoring responses to them, increasing their performance by appropriate development programs whether they work full or part-time, encouraging women to express rather than suppress their ambition, accepting part-time work and flexible arrangements at increasingly senior levels, and retaining good talent.

To do

✓ Ensure that diverse working practices are **available and supported.**

✓ Reconsider work organising principles and **promote new, flexible ways of working to outcomes.**

✓ Provide **infrastructure and enabling technology** that supports diverse work practices.

✓ Ensure that jobs and development opportunities are as available to those who work flexibly **as those who don't.** Create a target for the number of flexible workers who participate in general development programs or **create a target for each development program for flexible workers.**

✓ Provide specific **support/programs for parents.**

✓ Ensure the full array of options is available for **flexible re-engagement following leave.**

✓ Give priority to women moving back to ensure they are **not being sidelined in a 'part-time job'** – include this data in organizational reporting.

4.2 DIVERSE PRACTICES & CAREER PROGRESS COMPATIBLE

Despite the rhetoric of flexible work arrangements, it is clear that in some organizations there is a reluctance to embrace them, and a continuing belief that management roles and part-time work are not compatible. Even once women return to work from leave and actively seek further promotion, they may be unsupported in doing so.

Many top organizations espouse diversity as an organizational value, yet many diversity practices such as flexible work arrangements do little to support women's careers. Informal practices constrain the way in which women use the diversity provisions that are available in organizations. In one organization, management acknowledged the organization's masculine norms and values, but there was little attempt to surface and challenge the powerful informal practices that reinforced them, highlighting a 'hypocrisy gap'. While 55% of managers in one study reported that their organization provides flexible work provisions as an ethical requirement, only 30% said they actually deliver them. Organizations can support flexible work practices by avoiding marginalizing the careers of those who use them.

"Is it career or family? Let's make it both."
Andrew Stevens, Former MD, IBM A&NZ

Child rearing responsibilities generally coincide with moves into middle level managerial roles, yet the increased time commitments and pressures of middle management are seen as incompatible with women's family responsibilities. Family responsibilities are seen as barriers to women's availability for work, and availability is considered essential for promotion. There is an implicit assumption that working part-time is an indication of a lack of ambition; women's ambition is assumed to inevitably disappear once they have children.

In a European research study, women were more likely to have moved into managerial positions where they had received early support from colleagues and bosses or where they had worked closely with a more senior woman. The relationship with the manager is a key contributor: if managers actively enable flexible options to be taken and support their ongoing use, women's satisfaction increases.

Putting in long working hours is seen to be a critical part of being visible amongst a group of similarly experienced and capable performers. Executives are expected to be available at any time, including late at night and on weekends, and advances in technology including a burgeoning array of small portable devices make such availability increasingly common. Hours at work remains a crucial indicator of contribution, and while this is the case, women (and men) opting for flexible arrangements are disadvantaged. Especially in the arena of knowledge work, assessing people's relative contributions can be difficult. Where the focus can be shifted to more objective measures of productivity, women who have family responsibilities and effective and productive work habits can be more appropriately recognized for their contribution.

Women who are committed to their careers and seek to improve their status may nevertheless be seen as less committed by the organization if they take advantage of flexible work arrangements and family friendly opportunities.

In a UK study, executive women were clear that working reduced hours was perceived by others as a lack of career commitment. Some women were too afraid to even raise the issue of reduced hours because they believed they would then be excluded from promotional opportunities. In that same organization, junior male managers were scathing about women in management, not because of work performance, but because they were perceived to work shorter hours.

In a study of senior men and women in a European company, women responded to the need to be 'extensively available' in three main ways: one group of women acceded to the organizational requirements and put career first, usually at the expense of relationships and these women were more likely to be childless. A second group of women put home and family life first, working part time: they were considered to have opted out of their careers. A third group, who were generally in egalitarian personal relationships, attempted to combine the aspiration of career progression and quality family life. This group attempted to promote 'flexible availability' by working extremely efficiently and productively, drawing attention away from time and toward competence, performance and results. At home, they shared the outsourced management of domestic tasks as well as quality family interaction relatively equally with their partners. This pattern also seemed to appeal well to men in dual career couples and who took their wife's career requirements into consideration.

At Deloitte in 2000, flexible work arrangements were available, but a belief remained that working fewer hours would doom careers, and so they were rarely used. As a consequence of their diversity strategy, Deloitte reviewed the tough schedules consultants worked, and made adjustments to expectations about working away from home: they scaled back what they called their 'macho schedule of grinding travel'. The realization was reached that there had been a collective silence about the sacrifice that everyone made; they also discovered that everyone held work-life balance as an important goal. Once the sacrifices were made transparent and a less challenging schedule introduced, employees were happier, as were most customers who benefitted from a less hectic schedule themselves. In 2010 Deloitte received a Catalyst award for their ongoing dedication to the advancement of women.

Hays supports senior women in management holding flexible and part-time managerial roles. They have achieved 52% female managers, 62% of staff in part-time positions and 15% of part-time staff hold senior managerial roles. IBM Australia pioneered a job share arrangement for two senior women returning from parental leave and who both wanted to work part-time. They jointly manage a team of approximately 70 people. The shared role enables them to maintain their career goals. Telstra in 2014 launched an "All Roles Flex" initiative to highlight that the organization was open to discussing and implementing flexible options for every role.

European research highlights the connection between gender diversity programs and organizational productivity. Australian organizations reported that part-time managers were particularly focused, productive, and demonstrated higher loyalty to the organization in return for its flexibility and investment in them. If more women (and men) are satisfied with the flexible arrangements they make use of they will develop greater commitment to the organization. Commitment increases productivity and retention. Overall the talent pipeline is improved and there is greater likelihood of more women at senior levels.

Presence, or hours spent at work, continues to be a key driver of career success. Organizations that challenge this myth and focus instead on productivity and capability will unlock further potential in their talented staff.

> ### *To do*
>
> ✓ Encourage the use of flexible arrangements by senior leaders and men. **Work flexibly yourself.**
>
> ✓ Set **career progression rate targets** for women who have returned from maternity leave, promote stories of such women, their progress and success.
>
> ✓ Examine and **challenge the barriers** that exist to career advancement that usually accompany diverse working practices.
>
> ✓ Ensure that the **focus for performance is on outputs** and outcomes, not simply presence or hours at work.
>
> ✓ **Encourage flexible arrangements** to be supported and used by everyone with an individually tailored approach, and promote case stories that share the link to increased motivation and satisfaction.

4.3 INCLUSIVE GROUP DYNAMICS MANAGED

The promise of diversity in teams is an innovation dividend that comes from new and diverse information being introduced, processed and elaborated, increased discussion and integration of different ideas, increased error detection, and better group problem solving.

> *"Programs are the first stage in making a difference. Managers being accountable for the diversity of their teams and eliminating behaviour that is unacceptable is the next stage of driving cultural change."*
> Stephen Fitzgerald, former Chairman, Goldman Sachs A&NZ

But people prefer to work with similar others. We have an affinity bias, that is, it is more comfortable to work with people who are most like us. When diversity is introduced into homogenous groups, social identity may be disrupted. Subgroups emerge, and they create 'faultlines'. Subgroups can interfere with the sharing of information and they may create tension and conflict, which can interfere with the ability to tap into the resources that all group members bring.

Open self-expression creates greater satisfaction and a stronger social fabric within a team and an organization. Yet many women, and other minorities, often feel unable to fully and freely express themselves at work.

In male-dominated team contexts, power imbalances undermine psychological safety for women.

The ability to participate is not equal. Where power imbalances are not carefully managed, an individual's full potential may not be realized and the value of teamwork reduces. The following model provides a way to understand the dynamics of working in diverse teams, and highlights the contributions that good leadership can make to team functioning.

Figure 5. Inclusive team leadership model

4.3.1 Establish safety

In male-dominated organizations, professions and work teams, women may feel identity threat: their identity is called into question because they are different. Identity threat is the fear of being judged and treated unfairly, based on gender: 'You're a girl, you aren't good at maths', 'You're a woman, you aren't meant to be a leader'.

Identity threat occurs where gender is primed, or made salient. Priming is incredibly subtle and often unconscious. All it takes to prime for gender is having tick boxes for male or female on a form, and identity threat may follow. A male-dominated context primes gender. Having bosses or peers who express sexist attitudes primes a focus on gender and on gender stereotypes, and makes stereotypes salient.

Women respond to this priming by unconsciously shifting their behaviour in line with gender stereotypes. In organizational and performance contexts, they may lower their performance expectations so that they fall in line with stereotypical expectations. "I'm not meant to be a leader, therefore I'm not good at leading".

Negative thoughts about capabilities can cause an increase in performance anxiety. Trying to control the anxiety depletes mental resources. Attempts to counteract negative messages involve significant mental resources, which are then not available to the task at hand.

Attempting to suppress negative thoughts about performance and the associated anxiety appears to increase their power. Paradoxically, negative thoughts become hyper-accessible when suppressed.

Identity threat has a greater impact on women who have a higher level of concern for their status, who care the most about their maths or leadership skills, or how well they do on tests: their greater anxiety magnifies the reduction in mental resources available for the task. Identity threat also impacts most highly on women who consciously agree with gender stereotypes.

Performance therefore reduces, because there is less 'cognitive space' available for the task, and this reinforces stereotypes, 'You're a girl so you aren't good at maths'.

This kind of response is not just a response that women experience, but one that applies to all 'minds under threat'.

Women have a tendency to avoid situations that are male-dominated, as they don't see themselves fitting in. The need to fit and to belong is a fundamental psychological need and one that impacts significantly on women's choice of career, their interest in promotion, and their ability to project themselves into the most senior level leadership roles.

Identity threat does more than increase anxiety and decrease performance, it can also lead women to limit the choices they make about career options that require them to join male-dominated environments.

Priming can also be positive. Where women are primed to see themselves as particularly bright and capable, their performance is at least as good on maths tasks compared with men.

And women asked to imagine themselves as professors, later rate themselves as smarter. By imagining themselves in the professor role, their self-perceptions incorporate the stereotypical characteristics of the role. It also changes their behaviour; women playing the role of professor actually improved their analytical skills on a task undertaken after they had ceased playing the role.

As professions and work organizations become gender-balanced, negative stereotyping and categorization reduces. For example, the introduction of women into male-dominated symphony orchestras was initially very difficult. It only occurred when blind auditions were held. Initially, the increased presence of women led to declines in orchestra member satisfaction and social functioning. When the proportion of women reached around 30%, the initial dissatisfaction reversed.

Where there are social power differentials, identity threat means that non-dominant group members may not contribute at their maximum. Whether or not the full talents and capabilities of women are contributed in groups depends on their perceptions of how safe it is to be in the group.

In groups, it is assumed that work norms and styles are shared but in reality they favour the dominant group, here, men. Appealing to what is 'common' or 'shared' may diminish the contributions of women members, even if it is a well-intentioned attempt to create comfort and be welcoming.

Identity safety is assured where the non-dominant group members believe that their gender (or racial or cultural) identity is welcome in the group: this allows the creation of trust and comfort amongst group members.

The leader's role in a diverse group is to create psychological safety: to pay attention to the safety of team members and to actively create and maintain the conditions that minimize identity threat, providing security.

Coupled with this is the expression of 'diversity perspective' which is the explicit acknowledgement that diversity makes a positive contribution, that individuals' foundational identities shape life experience and have relevance for work. A diversity perspective welcomes diversity, seeing it as a sustaining factor that leads to the surfacing of new ideas. The leader names and relies on diversity in the team to contribute to team functioning and performance, and advocates its importance to the team's work.

The greater the psychological safety created in the team, the more likely diverse members are to feel identity safety and to feel congruent – 'I am seen by other group members in the same way that I see myself: the things that I cherish about myself, that I hold central to who I am, can be expressed in the group'. Greater personal congruence increases personal disclosure. Increased personal disclosure makes the team dynamic more productive. The more productive the team dynamic, the greater its effectiveness.

4.3.2 Manage diversity salience

The second element of the model focuses on the extent to which the team can actively work with its differences. There are two factors that apply here.

The combined factors of team members' levels of Openness to Experience (OE) and the salience of diversity within the team moderates whether or not the team is able to work with the diversity within it. The team leader has a critical role to assess the team's composition, understand the level of OE and make a strategic choice about what to do.

Figure 6. Openness to Experience Factors

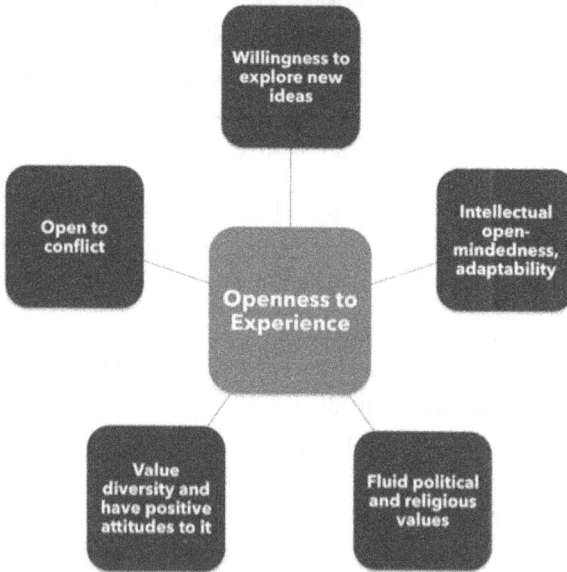

People high in OE promote discussion, exchange and elaboration of knowledge, insights and ideas relevant to the task, enabling a thorough and elaborate processing of diverse information. This results in increased opportunity to detect errors, increasing the amount of information processed, helps group problem solving and contributes to innovation. Where the group is high in OE and likes to work with difference and newness, the salience of diversity should be magnified.

Where individuals in the group are not high in OE, reducing the salience of diversity is a more productive tactic.

Diversity salience is reduced by creating a super-ordinate identity for the group. This reduces subgroup differences. Group reward structures, where meaningful rewards are provided to team members' on the basis of the team's achievements, is one of the most powerful ways to do this.

Rewarding a team based on team outcomes decreases the salience of intergroup differences and emphasizes the superordinate identity of the team. How do we all work together to achieve our goals?

The best team performance comes from a reward structure that cross cuts gender diversity and where individual members are high in OE.

Where there is a mix of people high and low in OE, cross cutting, that is, identifying as many kinds of diversity in the group as possible, is another way to reduce the salience of difference and to reduce bias and conflict between subgroups.

The worst performing teams are those where there is a diversity faultline (differences between subgroups are maximized) and members score low on OE.

4.3.3   Promote learning

Finally, can the group not just work with its differences but capitalize on them?

High value learning frames build on diversity perspectives and psychological safety, turning the acceptance of difference into innovation. The 'heat' in the group caused through diverse perspectives is moderated and an optimum zone for performance is managed.

A high learning frame means that team members advocate their own points of view as well as inquire into the view points of others: they are interested and curious about working with the varying perspectives in the team. In such a context, there is active debate and the team can work constructively with disagreement and conflict. 'Undiscussables', the tacit conflicts that are forbidden territory because they are 'too hot to handle' often remain unaddressed in teams and impede full engagement. Raising them means they might be used productively. Members with high learning frames are comfortable taking risks to create high value learning opportunities.

Low Learning Frame	High Learning Frame
Mistakes are crimes to be punished	Mistakes are puzzles to be engaged
I have a complete picture of this situation	Other people may have information or understanding I lack
I don't have anything to learn from others in this group	I can learn from others
If I don't have a solution, I shouldn't raise the problem	It is helpful to raise problems even if I don't have a solution
If I feel uncomfortable in this discussion, something must be wrong	Just because I feel uncomfortable in this conversation doesn't mean I shouldn't stick with it
Speaking up invites criticism	I have something to say and should contribute, even though I may be criticized
I'm powerless in this group, so I will be quiet	I can make a contribution even though I don't have any formal power or authority

If group members believe that their discomfort with risky topics signals a learning opportunity, they will be more likely to tolerate it. High learning frames authorize reflection about one's own point of view and curiosity about others.

If group members believe that their discomfort with risky topics signals a learning opportunity, they will be more likely to tolerate it. High learning frames authorize reflection about one's own point of view and curiosity about others.

How do you work with conflict, tolerate dissent, raise undiscussables and survive, let alone achieve great outcomes? Some intriguing recent research highlights the kinds of behaviour that supports working in this challenging area.

In very recent research on teams, those with more women achieved a 40% performance dividend. Collective Intelligence (CI) was a new term created to account for this effect.

Collective Intelligence refers to the extent to which teams are inclusive in making and integrating strategic decisions, and their ability to create connection within the group: the creation of a 'collective mind'.

Performance in the groups studied was not significantly related to either the average IQ of group members, or to the IQ of the smartest person in the team. It was also not related to group cohesion, motivation and satisfaction, traditionally considered important for teamwork.

Figure 7. Evidence for Collective Intelligence

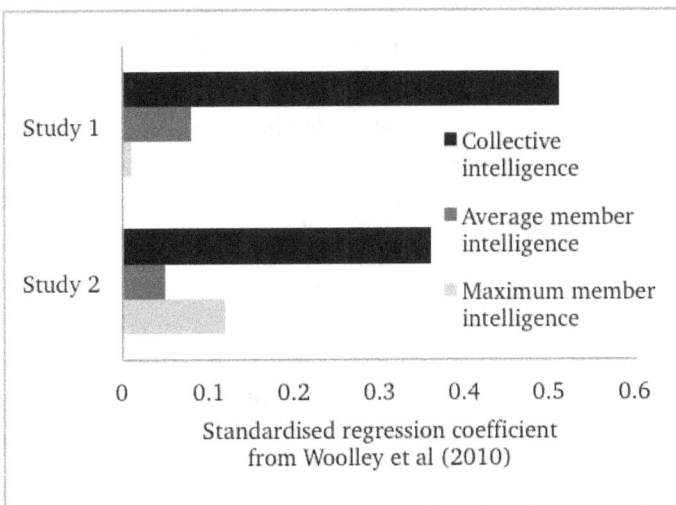

Standardised regression coefficient
from Woolley et al (2010)

The behaviours that characterised CI were the behaviours that women traditionally exhibit, such as accurately reading nonverbal cues, making accurate inferences about what others are thinking or feeling, equality of conversation which means that members are responsive to each other and make the best use of the knowledge and skills of members. They foster greater collaboration and cooperation. Women are much more interpersonally oriented, more democratic and focused on participation. They promote equal turn taking in conversation. They are more likely to shift performance contingencies in dynamic situations. Finally, women smile more whether they are speaking or listening, generating a warm, positive environment.

Men typically tend to display greater social dominance in groups, including gesturing, direct eye contact and chin thrusting, more autocracy and order giving, and this reduces collective action.

The upshot is that this behaviour enables the best use of the knowledge and skills of members: team members participate more, and more evenly.

In distinction to individual intelligence, the researchers claim that CI can be changed, by changing the composition of the group, providing incentives to group members to demonstrate greater social sensitivity, and increase inclusion and turn-taking. In gender diverse groups men and women behave more similarly. (Both men and women feel more positive about the group experience and there is a greater sense of efficacy and better morale when there are heterogeneous members.)

In summary, the leader promotes the learning behaviours of advocating, inquiring, surfacing undiscussables, and reflection, and pays attention to group processes that are associated with CI, such as collaboration, equal turn-taking and responsiveness.

Adding a token woman to a team in a male-dominated context may decrease performance and team relationships. Clustering women in teams in such contexts, rather than spreading them across teams is a better way to introduce women, break down limiting stereotypes, increase positive experiences and achieve the performance benefits of Collective Intelligence.

> **To do**
>
> ✓ Provide managers with training and assistance in **managing the dynamics of diverse teams.**

Checklist of Work practices

Identify the extent to which your organization has implemented the following actions, using the rating system:

1. We already do this well

2. In train, with room for improvement

3. We don't do this, or do it poorly

Work Practices	Rating
4.1 Diverse practices supported	
• Ensure that diverse working practices are available and supported. • Reconsider work organising principles and promote new, flexible ways of working to outcomes. • Provide infrastructure and enabling technology that supports diverse work practices. • Ensure that jobs and development opportunities are as available to those who work flexibly as those who don't. Create a target for the number of flexible workers who participate in general development programs or create a target for each development program for flexible workers. • Provide specific support/programs for parents. • Ensure the full array of options is available for flexible re-engagement following leave. • Give priority to women moving back into their prior role to ensure they are not being sidelined in a 'part-time job' – include this data in organisational reporting.	

Work Practices	Rating
4.2 Diverse practices and career progress compatible	
• Encourage the use of flexible arrangements by senior leaders and men. Work flexibly yourself. • Set career progression rate targets for women who have returned from maternity leave, promote stories of such women, their progress and success. • Examine and challenge the barriers that exist to career advancement that usually accompany diverse working practices. • Ensure that the focus for performance is on outputs and outcomes, not mere presence or hours at work. • Encourage flexible arrangements to be supported and used by everyone with an individually tailored approach, and promote case stories that share the link to increased motivation and satisfaction.	
4.3 Inclusive group dynamics managed	
• Provide managers with training and assistance in managing the dynamics of diverse teams.	

What are three key actions that would help progress Work Practices in your organisation?

1. _____

2. _____

3. _____

5.

FAIR TALENT AND PERFORMANCE MANAGEMENT

"Women are Australia's hidden resource. The gains that we could make as a country by elevating the representation of women in leadership is substantial. We are a long way from realizing the full potential of our workforce. We need to make this a priority."
~ Stephen Fitzgerald, former Chairman,
Goldman Sachs A&NZ

Women experience disadvantage when it comes to talent and performance management. Compared with men, women are less likely to be promoted into managerial roles, under-estimate their readiness for increased responsibility and are less likely to make it into the high potential talent pool or on the succession list. They are less likely to have access to key developmental opportunities that assist promotional opportunities. Women have their achievements acknowledged less, get lower performance ratings and are paid less for the same work. More transparent talent identification, development and recognition practices will increase fairness of opportunity.

5.1 TALENT IDENTIFICATION

"Women in Australia are an under-utilized resource. We need to be tapping more heavily into the other half of the resource pool. It's that simple."
Stephen Roberts, CEO, Citi Australia

Review 5.1: Assess your organization's progress: How fair are your organization's talent identification processes?

✔✔✔	Transparent checks and balances are in place to ensure that all decision points that define, identify and select talent provide fair opportunity to both genders
✔✔	There is a concern to ensure that talent programs are not biased, but there is no systematic review process in place
✔	Managers are responsible for making talent decisions for their team members
✗	There are no clear accountabilities for talent management

5.1.1 Identifying potential

Even with formal talent identification policies and processes many organizations don't implement checks and balances to ensure that gender assumptions are minimized, resulting in new senior leaders who mirror the same styles and preferences as the preceding senior leaders.

This can translate into organizations' competency models and other talent management tools and so create disadvantage for women by projecting typically masculine behaviours as requirements for promotion. As a consequence talent pools are diluted.

The identification of high potentials is often focused on the age group 28-35 years, when women are most likely to be starting their families: extending the age profile and considering capability rather than age and increasing the flexibility of high potential development programs may all serve to increase the engagement of women and maximize talent development.

Sensitizing managers to potential biases in identifying potential is also important. A number of organizations now suggest ensuring that every shortlist for selection has at least one woman, which goes some way to overcoming the barriers experienced and sensitizes line managers to the possibilities of engaging women.

Royal Bank of Canada's approach includes ensuring that succession pools are diverse and its targets include equal numbers of women being promoted into executive and management roles. They provide coaching and development plans for talented women who miss out on promotions. Between 2005 and 2009, they significantly increased the representation of women in their high potential program.

Figure 8. Women in Royal Bank of Canada's high potential pool

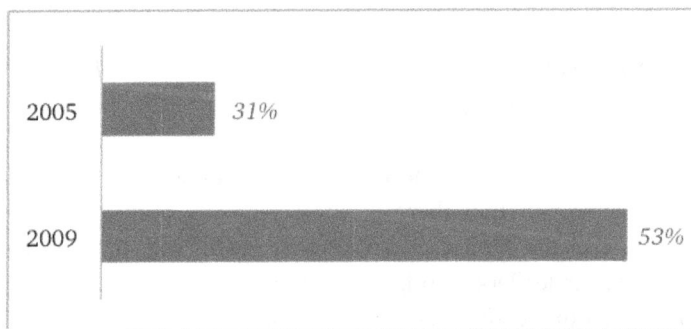

Finance sector organizations generally report the active identification and promotion of high potential females.

Fair selection and promotion is based on identification of talent that comes in many forms, making decision processes transparent, recognizing the different approaches and preferences of different genders, and being responsive to both.

To do
✓ Audit and **adjust leadership competencies** to be gender neutral.
✓ **Review talent guidelines,** raise awareness of the possibility of subtle bias and institute audits to **ensure gender-free talent reviews.**
✓ Ensure **equal gender targets** in succession and high potential programs. Ensure these talent processes are open to scrutiny and that decision-making has clear criteria.
✓ Support women as they join **the succession pool.**
✓ When high potential women miss out on promotions, conduct an objective review of processes and outcomes and **provide them with comprehensive feedback for development** and support to close gaps.

5.1.2 Leadership talent

Leadership roles occupy premium position in organizations, bestowing authority and legitimizing rules and appropriate behaviour. Leadership roles drive norms that regulate behaviour throughout the organization. Research has shown that there is an incongruity between the female gender role and the typical organizational leader role that creates bias against women in leadership roles and this is fully explored in Section 3.1.5. Judgments about women being less able to fulfill leadership role requirements and lower evaluations of their performance as leaders are routine.

Despite these norms, female leaders have been shown to demonstrate a range of behaviours well suited to leadership roles, including greater social and emotional intelligence. Women demonstrate the leadership behaviours of inspiration, participatory decision-making, and expectation and reward setting to a greater extent than do men. In an analysis of the responses of more than 20,000 managers in a European business school study, women were assessed more highly on eight out of ten key leadership attributes; both men's and women's assessments of female leaders were in agreement, in the cases of male and female superiors and subordinates. In the case of peers, males gave the women much lower scores.

"The success of our strategy depends on having a vibrant workforce, with people who understand and can connect with our customers and markets wherever we operate. With more women in our leadership pipeline and senior executive ranks, we are tapping into a much broader range of leadership styles, experiences and skills to manage our business and achieve our goals."
Michael Smith, CEO, ANZ Banking Group Ltd

In a significant study, Eagly, Johannesen-Schmidt and Van Engen meta-analysed 55 studies of leadership to examine whether perceptions of women's and men's leadership styles differed and if so, whether women's leadership styles might assist or inhibit their progression to more senior roles. The studies measured transformational, transactional and laissez-faire leadership styles, primarily as measured by the Multifactor Leadership Questionnaire, and based on 360° feedback. This model of leadership has undergone substantial global research, demonstrating the transformational style as the strongest contributor to leadership success.

The meta-analysis showed that female leaders were significantly more transformational than male leaders. They were seen to motivate pride and respect in others, exhibit optimism and confidence about the organization's future, examine new perspectives and focus on development and mentoring more than men. Women were also scored more highly than men on the transactional subscale of recognizing good performance.

Male leaders scored higher than female leaders on the transformational leadership subscale of communicating purpose and the importance of mission. Male leaders were significantly more transactional, scoring higher on acting promptly to deal with mistakes and waiting until problems arose before intervening. They were also more laissez-faire than female leaders.

Transformational style
<ul><li>Motivates respect and pride in others</li><li>Communicates purpose and the importance of mission and values</li><li>Exhibits optimism and confidence about the organisation's future</li><li>Examines new perspectives for solving problems and completing tasks</li><li>Focuses on development and mentoring of employees and considers their individual needs</li></ul>
Transactional style
<ul><li>Recognises good performance</li><li>Acts promptly to deal with employees' mistakes and failures</li><li>Waits until problems arise before intervening</li></ul>
Laissez-faire style
<ul><li>Frequently absent</li><li>Lacks involvement during critical projects and events</li></ul>

The findings of this meta-analysis were compared by McKinsey's in organizational research that found more women to be associated with better organizational performance. The researchers attributed the better organizational performance to increased transformational behaviour associated with more women in leadership roles.

Women's transformational leadership style contributes to better organizational performance.

Eagly and her co-authors conclude that if organizations open their talent pools more widely to women, they do more than simply increase the size of the pool and create greater fairness, they also increase the capability of the pool, adding superior leadership capability. Yet, knowledge that women have the right leadership styles to assist organizations, particularly in uncertain times, has not led to an increase in their promotion to senior roles, and so women experience leadership advantage and disadvantage.

Besides the gender belief, Eagly and Johanessen speculate that there may also be resistance by male executives to changing leadership styles.

Organizations that broaden their acceptance of a full range of leadership styles, open talent pools to women and men who demonstrate transformational leadership, and promote women into senior leadership roles, achieve better outcomes.

To do

✓   Assess the organisation's definition of leadership and review the competency model to **avoid a masculine depiction of leadership** and instead offer a wide range of leadership capabilities and styles.

✓   As part of leadership development programs, **highlight responsibility for gender equity** and the value of diversity.

5.1.3   Barriers removed

"How do we change the way we select, recruit, induct to overcome that unconscious bias within an organization that may lead us down a more narrow recruitment and development path."
Cameron Clyne, former CEO, NAB

A key barrier to progress is stereotyping, which leads to biased decision-making, which is addressed comprehensively in Chapter 3. Stereotypes about leadership are responsible for narrow definitions that foster a focus on sameness rather than difference and that reinforce male dominance, contributing to low numbers of women on executive teams. Women are more likely to believe stereotyping limits their progress than men are. Bias limits the likelihood that women will be selected for senior roles. And it also leads to women self-selecting out of leadership roles, by judging their readiness for roles more harshly, reducing their ambition and making more limited career choices.

Women managers are seen to lack self-confidence, or at least have a lower level of confidence than men do: men and women seek advancement opportunities in different ways and at different levels of readiness. Women are less likely than men to consider themselves suitable for promotion. Women tend to apply for senior roles if they consider that they meet 100% of the selection criteria, whereas men apply if they think they meet 60% of requirements. Seventy percent of women rate their own performance as equivalent to their co-workers while 70% of men rate themselves higher than their co-workers. Whether women have a lack of confidence, or a different way of engaging that gives the appearance of a lack of confidence, is a matter of conjecture.

Not only are women disadvantaged when they behave in different ways to men, women are labelled differently for demonstrating the same behaviour as men.

Assertiveness is seen as normal and acceptable in men and less so in women. Women who put themselves forward for promotional opportunities tend to be seen as pushy or worse, while men are seen as 'go-getters' and 'straight shooters' when they engage in the same behaviour. This is a challenge, as active self-promotion is generally considered a key to success.

While these perception barriers may help to explain why more men are promoted than women it certainly doesn't help to explain why organizations continue to listen to male and female voices in a way that is almost certainly disadvantageous to the organization. More awareness training for managers so that they can translate these differences meaningfully is called for. Best practice organizations raise awareness that men and women have different patterns of behaviour, seek out competent women for opportunities, and shift the culture so that it welcomes women actively seeking to build their own careers and assertively putting themselves forward for advancement opportunities. At the same time, managers learn not to simply equate men's self-promotion with competence, and more actively test their readiness.

To do

✓ Provide or advocate for **training for managers in awareness and impact of bias**, recognising the different behaviours of men and women, having career conversations, and thinking creatively about ways to engage women in their careers while balancing family responsibilities.

5.1.4   Same rate of progress

Women's slower progression rate is in many ways an outcome of the biases in selection, promotion and development noted above.

The evidence is clear that promotions come more slowly for women than for men with equivalent qualifications, with one study showing 72% of CEOs and 51% of female executives consider that gender assumptions are a significant impediment to advancement. In another study two thirds of men and just under one third of women believe there is an equal chance of being promoted to executive roles on the same time-line. Lesser skills, education and time out of the workforce have been ruled out as explanatory for the differential progression rates.

Not only do women progress at a slower rate than men, they usually progress one step of the ladder at a time and are more likely to move laterally than men, who focus with greater vigilance on their rate of progress and may be supported in skipping steps. Women reach senior management later than men. In one study there were a few women who were exceptions, and these women had a 'special' quality of some kind, such as a degree from a highly prestigious university or school, possession of rare expertise or the cachet of having worked at an organization with a highly prestigious brand.

There is a strong correlation between progression rate and age. High potentials are generally on the fast track by 35 years of age and have commenced their first senior management role by the time they are 50, a progression rate that implies constant work involvement, no career breaks and avoidance of organizational hazards or career dead-ends. High visibility and extensive availability require a high degree of self-sacrifice and total devotion to career. This pattern is incompatible with the usual age at which women have children; the pattern not only presumes devotion to career, but generally presumes a supportive wife whose social capabilities are used not just in the home but also to assist her husband's career.

To avoid these patterns Hays instituted practices designed to enable women to make equitable progress. Their focus on merit ensured that in 2009 52% of high potentials identified through the Board's succession planning were women. Additionally 55% of participants in their Senior Management Development Centre were women.

Women who return to large corporates after taking time-out to pursue a non-traditional path (including but not limited to family responsibilities) advance more slowly than both men and women who stay on the traditional career path following their MBA.

Career progression rate is a complex issue. In organizations with few women at the top, junior women place limits on their likelihood of success and consequently lower their expectations and their confidence, in turn reducing the likelihood that they will put themselves forward for career opportunities. In organisations that demonstrate leading gender diversity practice, women and men have similar progression rates.

To do

- ✓ At or around age 30, **do a career review for all managerial, professional and high potential women,** providing expert career advice and the opportunity to discuss career aspirations and opportunities.

- ✓ Ensure that **key roles have either been undertaken or are planned,** to provide breadth in knowledge and experience.

- ✓ **Discuss family aspirations** and identify the barriers that might be encountered and how they could be overcome to maximise career success.

- ✓ **Assess the level of support that has been provided by line managers** and intervene in relationships that do not seem to be benefiting women.

5.2 RECRUITMENT AND SELECTION

Right from the start, women and men are treated differently, setting up differential expectations and experiences that shape and drive behaviour over careers.

"We know that a diverse workforce creates value and we need to ensure we reflect the customers and communities we work with. NAB sees our focus on the advancement of women as a never ending journey. Early progress has been pleasing, however, we need to ensure we stay the course."
Cameron Clyne, Former CEO, NAB

Review 5.2: Assess your organization's progress: Do men and women experience equal opportunity to be hired and promoted in your organization?

✔✔✔ We have instituted changes that mitigate against gender bias, and our data shows that women and men have equal opportunity to be hired and promoted

✔✔ We provide equal opportunity to men and women by making sure that there is at least one woman on the selection panel for all senior appointments

✔ Our data shows that men and women do not have equal opportunity to be hired and promoted into senior leadership roles and we are still working out what to do to change this

✗ Our managers are given the freedom to recruit best fit candidates

Women tend to be placed in lower starting grade levels than similar men who commence at the same time, creating a longer career path to the top. US male MBA graduates are more likely to begin their working career in a job with higher responsibilities than females. Eliminating biases from the start is important for valuing and maximising the talent of all staff.

While most organizations pride themselves on being meritocracies, the reality is that unconscious beliefs are at work during selection processes, and while they have a subtle impact on any one decision, the cumulative impact can create real disadvantage for women. While any one decision may not affect a specific person in a specific instance, the cumulative effect of bias across many decisions over time is significant.

> *"We need to get the best talent for our Firm. Everyone is competing for female talent and we aim to get more than our fair share. If we attract and retain great people, we succeed in better serving our clients. Without talent we can't serve our clients effectively."*
> Giam Swiegers, Former CEO, Deloitte

All other things being equal, for every 50 women and 50 men an organization should hire, the evidence demonstrates that it actually hires 58 women and 52 men and this compounds over successive decisions: after four decisions, there is a 16% difference in gender representation.

Figure 9. Cumulative effect of stereotypes on hiring decisions

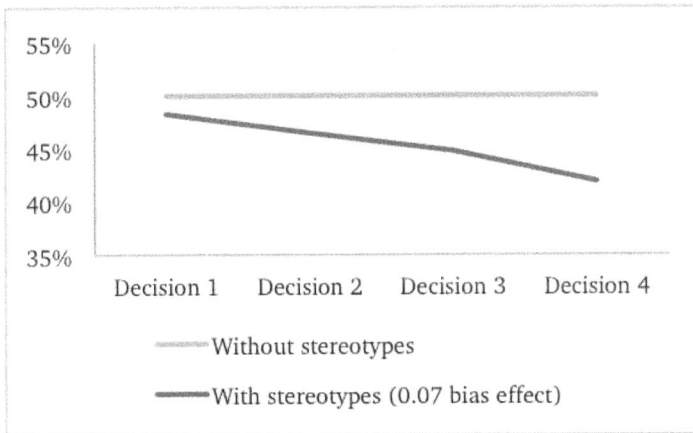

At higher organization levels, bias impact magnifies, as the distribution of managers is already skewed and evaluation is more open to assumptions. A further impact of this bias is that after each step in the process, the remaining sample of men are slightly less talented than the remaining sample of women, although generally this does not impact selection decisions, assuming that the most talented in the pool are selected.

Feike Sijbesma, Chairman of the Managing Board of Royal DSM considered that each new hiring decision was a point for action to improve gender equity. He increased the number of women on his supervisory board by consciously avoiding the relatively easy hiring of men, and deliberately looking for excellent female hires.

Informal selection processes usually restrict the talent pool, reducing merit and decreasing the likelihood of the best appointments being made.

Even prior to selection processes, external women need to be sufficiently attracted to roles in organizations in order to apply. In some cases, the image projected by organizations in their external advertisements has a significant impact on whether or not women apply. In one European organization, the percentage of female applicants applying for positions increased from 5% to 50% following changes to the advertisement from a man projecting aggression and competitiveness to a senior woman focusing on enthusiasm and innovation.

External selection is fair when organizations train those involved in making selection decisions and closely monitor the outcomes of decisions over time, ensuring that equal numbers of men and women are appropriately evaluated at each decision phase, and where equal numbers do not apply in the first place, responding innovatively to improve the balance.

The same assumptions impacting external selection outcomes apply to internal selection and promotion. Sixty-six percent of men believe that women have equal opportunity to be promoted to leadership and governance positions, but less than a third of women agree. Based on the small numbers of women on corporate executive teams, with 62% of ASX200 organizations not having any women on their team, more thoughtful work to develop truly fair processes is required.

For internal promotion and transfer processes to be fair, they need to account for a number of factors that impact unfairly on women: the visibility and isolation of 'token' women, the lack of role models demonstrating clear female professional identities, negative stereotypes about women's suitability for leadership roles, and women's disengagement from leadership aspiration. In addition, internal promotion for senior positions can be highly influenced by informal processes.

Women who do reach the top levels of organizations are less likely to be married or have children, to be in dual career relationships, are on average younger than their male counterparts, have been in their organizations longer, while men are more likely to have non-working spouses, providing further evidence of bias in selection.

To do

✓ Review recruitment and talent policies to **alert managers to communication and negotiation style differences.**

✓ Consider **reporting mechanisms for managers who fail to promote** a targeted percentage of women.

✓ Promote the CEO's involvement in all senior recruitment activities, driving a **deeper pool of female candidates,** not accepting less than equity, and not accepting the first candidate pool provided if it is not equitable.

✓ **Audit job descriptions and job advertisements** for bias and image. Increase awareness of the subtle impact of biases, put measures in place to avoid easy hiring decisions and use creative options for increasing the pool of female candidates.

✓ Create **transparent monitoring of numbers of women** at each recruitment decision point.

✓ **Increase the attractiveness of certain line roles,** e.g. by clustering women together to create a critical mass rather than distributing them thinly, which creates a barrier to women's participation.

5.3 DEVELOPMENT

"Sponsorship is about moving from coffee chats and advice, to actually backing our women, and feeling responsible for their career success. It's a real mindset shift."
Stephen Fitzgerald, former Chairman, Goldman Sachs A&NZ

Review 5.3: Assess your organization's progress: Are men and women given equal opportunity to develop their skills and capabilities?

✔✔✔ Men and women have equal access to the full range of development opportunities, including those that have high value for promotion

✔✔ There is awareness that men's and women's access to development opportunities is not equal and actions to improve access for women are being developed

✔ Development opportunities, particularly those at senior levels, continue to be dominated by men

✗ There is no available data on men and women's engagement in development activities

5.3.1 Sponsor support for development

More has been written about mentoring as a support mechanism in women's promotional prospects than just about any other topic. Yet the research on the value and payback from mentoring identifies circumstances where mentoring is beneficial, and others where it appears detrimental to future success.

Many formal mentoring programs are not effective. Perhaps appropriately then, Nesbit and Seeger reported a low take-up rate of mentoring programs in their in-depth study of 30 Australian organizations. In another study, women saw the mentoring available in their organizations as a

110

paper exercise by their mentors and considered it useless. Plugging in structured, formal mentoring programs in an effort to redress disadvantage in this way may not yield the expected benefits.

Traditionally, women received less mentoring than their male peers and mentoring was more strongly associated with men's career success than women's. Women without mentors progressed more slowly than men and than women who had mentors.

Both men and women are more likely to receive mentoring from successful men: for women receiving this benefit it provides access to valuable information and networks, yet it can also be complicated by traditional gender roles and expectations.

Senior women are reluctant to mentor other women because they feel too burdened, consider it risky for their own careers, or they doubt their qualifications.

Tharenou's empirical study of mentoring in Australian organizations found that it had greater career impact for women versus men, but only where it was explicitly focused on career advancement.

Mentoring focused on psychosocial support	Focuses on emotional wellbeing and personal growth, demonstrated as friendship, acceptance, counselling, role-modelling. Doesn't improve career advancement and may negatively impact salary and progression.
Mentoring focused on career advance-ment	Focuses on career advancement and sponsorship, enabling access to high profile assignments and coaching; provides visibility, credibility and legitimacy. Leads to increases in salary and promotion rate.

Recent international research shows that while women were slightly more likely than men to have a mentor, women's mentors held lower level managerial roles and, again, were more focused on psychosocial support. In contrast, men's mentors were more senior, which is associated with a faster rate of progression: men in the study were more likely to have taken steps up the ladder while women were more likely to have moved laterally. Men's mentors tended to focus on sponsorship, helping the men to plan their next moves, to take charge in new roles, and publicly endorsed them, thus legitimizing their authority.

To make better use of mentoring based on sponsorship Deutsche Bank created a program pairing women with executive committee mentors to provide them with influential advocates for their advancement. Unilever selected similar sponsors who took part in appointment decisions, with the intention of having advocates for the women at promotion time, and participants in Price Waterhouse Coopers' Building Female Leaders program were assigned a partner sponsor whose role was to assist them to attain leadership roles and have meaningful careers within the firm.

Mentoring also has benefits in increasing the acceptance of female leadership. Men who have had female mentors demonstrate greater awareness of gender assumptions.

Mentor support for career development, focusing on sponsorship, contributes to increased advancement, under certain circumstances. Organizations can reap the benefits of mentoring by assigning mentoring responsibility to senior executives, providing training for potential mentors on how to provide sponsorship and career advancement support. Likewise, opportunities for men to be mentored by women can contribute to a stronger appreciation of the assumptions that women face. Organizations can establish mentoring as a more transparent and open process, supporting senior women to contribute their expertise in mentoring both women and men. Assigning accountability for sponsorship outcomes also increases the rate of promotion for recipients.

> *To do*
>
> ✓ **Sponsor high potential** women.
> ✓ Provide and undertake training in **high quality mentorship**.

5.3.2 Fair access to high profile assignments

Women are less likely to be given access to specific experiences shown to be significant for leadership development and future career success, namely challenging work assignments, including international assignments, and assignments that carry a high risk for the organization. These experiences provide a high level of visibility.

Senior women have fewer international assignments than men. International assignments provide high visibility and build cross-cultural skills, and lead to success in more senior roles. In one study women expressed the same level of willingness to relocate for career enhancement or company need as men, although they were slightly more likely than men to identify restrictions, such as dual career needs and timing concerns.

"We undertake early and activist career and succession planning to ensure we are creating a strong pipeline for line and business roles."
Michael Smith, CEO, ANZ Banking Group Ltd

Geographical mobility tends to be a normal part of career progression. Within a Paris-based organization, where women refused mobility assignments either because of stability for the sake of their children or because their husband's career took precedence, their careers tended to stall. Without broader experience across the organization, they ended up in a narrow range of staff roles, with little prospect of promotion.

Most organizations do not have audit processes to identify whether high profile assignments are distributed without the influence of gender assumptions, nor the level of support that would enable women to more easily take on such assignments. Organizations might also consider more creative approaches that provide exposure to multiple parts of the business and build broader capabilities, in different kinds of ways.

In contrast to the foregoing, Ernst & Young Australia achieved just under 50% of international secondment opportunities being taken up by women in 2009, a key outcome of their diversity and inclusion program.

In the workplace, those people who create good positive relationships with their work colleagues are more likely to be promoted. Active support of colleagues, not just seeking help from them, creates strong social capital. Women and men must have strong social capital to be successful; and for women it takes greater effort to build it. Informal networks are a primary source of social capital. Men maintain their networks because they hold value for career progression. Men in general are better able to maintain valuable networks as they have fewer restrictions on their time availability after working hours. Women have less time available for work-related networking outside of regular business hours.

Fair access to high profile assignments and opportunities has the potential to ensure women's and men's talents are fully developed and contribute to organizational performance.

Women feel excluded from the influential networks that exist in organizations, and in the wider business world. They further believe that being excluded from informal networks limits their career opportunities. For women, networks with women, networks with men, mentors, and good relationships with superiors all contribute to building social capital. Generally, women have difficulty in joining networks dominated by men, but should not be daunted. Women who are able to cultivate networks and relationships with men get high value payback.

Enabling fair access to influential networks will assist in redressing this inherent imbalance in social capital development. ANZ bank has established a 'Notable Women' program to enable women greater access to business networks, business press and social media, as a way of helping them to achieve their full leadership potential and with the goal of increasing gender balance in senior leadership roles.

Women are also more likely to gain access to staff rather than line positions. Line positions with profit and loss responsibility more often lead to senior organizational roles. In a study of 1,000 US senior executives, lack of line management experience was seen by 79% of executive women and 90% of CEOs as the primary obstacle to women making it to senior roles.

Figure 10. Biggest barrier to advancement: Lack of general management or line experience

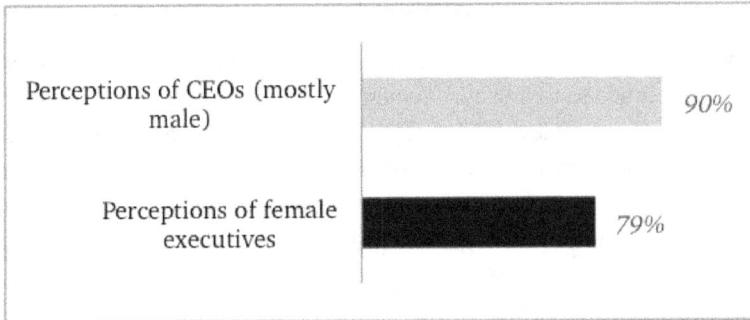

Perceptions of CEOs (mostly male) — 90%

Perceptions of female executives — 79%

Property developer Stockland identified that a key route to senior leadership roles involved experience within their Development function, and yet women were under-represented in these roles. In 2014 they commenced a program to both hire senior women into these roles, and develop a strong internal pipeline of female talent. They have focused on equality of opportunity from graduate intake through all organizational levels, with the goal of achieving gender equality in senior roles.

Organizations continue to under-promote women into key operational roles. Operational roles provide a broad exposure to the business, necessitate management of large staff cohorts, and require a deep understanding of financial management and accountabilities. These roles, more than any other role or experience, are the conduit to the executive suite. An examination of US Fortune 1000 companies found that women in line functions, with higher education and with experience in law were the most likely to make it to the top.

In 2010, Ernst & Young Australia reported that almost 57% of recruitment promotions into line management roles had been women. The Campbell Soup Company, which won a Catalyst Award in 2010, credits five years of dedicated attention to diversity for its significant business turnaround. Five years ago, Campbell's had stagnant sales and particularly poor employee engagement scores. As their primary consumers were women they made diversity a core focus for their turnaround. The percentage of women in executive roles increased from 21 to 25%, and there was a significant increase in women running major business lines, such that representation in manufacturing increased from 15 to 21%. Both profitability and employee engagement indicators saw dramatic improvement.

Organizations must unlock the assumptions that are getting in the way of women's fair access to line and managerial roles, and do that at lower and middle management levels. Only by doing this will the pipeline issues that continue to be blamed for women's under-representation be addressed: organizations with more women in top management positions also had more women in junior management positions.

To do

✓   **Prime women to understand and request developmental aspects in their job roles.**

✓   Audit and **monitor the distribution of high profile assignments** across gender and ensure access to high profile assignments for flexible workers.

✓   Support a **CEO forum for women in senior line management roles** to discuss business/operational issues, provide direct access to the CEO and other senior organisational champions.

✓   Encourage senior organisation leaders to **invite women into key networks** ensuring they are fully integrated into power groups.

✓   **Ensure high potential women are members of and develop influential networks,** facilitate introductions and build confidence.

5.3.3   Gender specific programs

Where women are in the minority they experience benefits from learning with other women and perceive the organization to be more supportive of them, making access to women only programs an important component in developing and retaining key female talent.

Female only development provides an environment that encourages risk taking, fosters collaborative learning and enables greater self-disclosure. It allows women to develop with authenticity.

Gender assumptions prevent women from developing to their full potential. Women may experience mixed-gender (i.e., male-dominated) development activities as competitive, based as they often are on male models of learning. Such development is less likely to meet women's needs. Women have little chance to learn with other women, they struggle to have the female voice heard and are often expected to undertake menial tasks as well as take responsibility for the group's social tasks. In such training, they can feel marginalized and unconnected, repeating their experiences of the work place.

Senior women identify support from other women as beneficial. It enables women to 'speak their own language' to someone who understands and helps avoid feeling like a foreigner.

There have been arguments against women only development, with perceptions that it is seen as a fix-it for women and perpetuates the biases against them: such programs rightly operate as complements, not replacements, to mixed-gender development.

In Nesbit and Seeger's Australian study, they found that only three of their 30 participating organizations offered women-only leadership training programs, despite those organizations identifying the need to overcome the perceived lower confidence and self-promotion of women as leaders. Westpac has a Women Achieving their Potential program for middle managers to assist them develop career plans and build their personal skills and effectiveness.

KPMG (Australia) provides a number of development opportunities for women, including career resilience programs, Executive Women's Development Program, and International Women's Day celebrations and

IBM Australia offers a similar array of programs for women at different organizational levels.

Ernst & Young Australia provides senior women's leadership forums to develop a sense of community amongst women.

Women participating in female-only leadership programs identify increased candour of discussions and the opportunity for greater self-disclosure as key benefits. The atmosphere of such development is collaborative rather than competitive, with a focus on finding common ground. Participants are able to identify shared experiences and learn relationally. Women only networks assist in creating opportunities for women to achieve broader exposure, raise their profiles and identify with role models.

The University of Western Australia has provided a Leadership Development for Women program for 15 years. Evaluations of the impact of the program show that graduates of the program have better retention and promotion rates than women who don't participate and than men.

IBM Australia fosters or supports a series of networking activities for women, focusing on enabling women to progress in the heavily male-dominated IT industry.

They provide a global women's forum, an Australia/New Zealand networking group, sponsor a global women's organization dedicated to advancing women in IT and link women to technical and senior level leaders to support their development through networking.

Through providing women's leadership development activities, organizations establish a positive context in which women experience the benefits of women-only development, as one of a range of career building opportunities.

Achieving gender diversity targets requires the shared efforts of both men and women. As women negotiate entry to and ownership of leadership roles in organizations, so too must men negotiate norms that govern their behaviour. Men's engagement in discussions about gender, including masculine norms, is a determinant in whether or not they support or oppose gender equity programs.

In Catalyst's research, they found that one of the most effective ways of enabling men to think critically about gender was through facilitated, male-only discussions about gender. This enabled the men to understand the reality and impact of gender beliefs, to discuss what they see as its personal costs, to explore potential personal benefits from better gender diversity, and to understand how to develop better relationships with women colleagues.

Ernst & Young in 2006 chose to engage men more closely in their diversity program. Focus groups were held in the US and Canada with the purpose of better understanding male perspectives in the firm. These conversations led to firm-wide leadership dialogues between men and women focusing on inequities, biases and the personal costs of gender equity for both women and men, as well as local workshops in business units to engage partners on key issues and to develop locally-owned strategies and action plans that are embedded in management processes.

These discussions increase men's awareness of gender assumptions and increase the likelihood that they will then believe it is important to achieve gender equality. Almost all men who are aware of gender assumptions believe that it is important to achieve equity.

More than that, research on off-shore oil rigs, bastions of macho behaviour, indicate that firstly, shifting such macho behaviour is possible, and secondly, minimizing macho behaviour is vital to achieving top performance.

Best practice organizations provide the opportunity for men to engage in men-only discussions about gender.

> ### To do
>
> ✓ Provide a range of **gender-specific programs.**
>
> ✓ Provide networking/skills development programs for **younger women** to introduce them to the leadership domain and build their confidence and ambition as future leaders.
>
> ✓ Provide **women's only development programs and networks for middle and senior women** to develop strategies for being a part of the dominant paradigm.

5.4 RETENTION

Negative stereotypes about women's suitability for leadership mean some women disengage from their leadership aspirations and more women leave organizations dissatisfied than men do.

Review 5.4: Assess your organization's progress: Are there differences in retention rates and patterns for men and women?

✓✓✓	Turnover rates of men and women at all levels of the organization are the same
✓✓	Higher turnover rates for women in middle and senior roles have been identified and strategies identified to reduce them
✗	We do not have reliable data on turnover rates
✗	Women leave the workforce to have families and so it makes sense that they have a higher turnover rate

Female turnover reduces once women achieve junior management roles, significantly increases at middle management level and then decreases slightly at senior levels. Larger companies experience higher levels of turnover, and companies with more activities devoted to the inclusion of women experience lower turnover.

> *"Programs are important. They take you on a journey. However, for more progress, more is needed. When you see something that is wrong, for example, attrition, you have to ask yourself, "What's wrong?" and be willing to fix it. This takes an approach that is broader than programs."*
> David Thodey, CEO, Telstra

Women see the lack of senior women at the very top of their organizations as a lack of a meritocracy in promotion and a lack of support for their development organisational leaders believe strongly in the importance of meritocracy, yet fewer are aware of how fragile it is and that it is not necessarily a shared experience.

In US Fortune 1000 companies, turnover of women from top teams (where they constituted 5% of those teams) was 33% compared with 19% for men. Interestingly, in those same companies, the greater the age difference between (younger) women and (older) men, the greater the turnover of women.

Relative power is a major factor influencing whether or not an executive will stay in the organization. Competent women stay where they feel powerful, have the respect of their peers and direct reports and are integrated into the dominant power group.

Deloitte Consulting's former CEO was aware of talented women leaving the firm but he and his fellow senior partners assumed they were doing so to have children and stay at home. They were not aware that many of those women were going to rival firms who provided greater support for flexibility, in order to progress their careers.

Women's commitment to their organizations is largely associated with their perception of the support they receive from their managers. That commitment is eroded where managers do not listen and value women, and related to this, where they lack support in achieving the work-life balance they desire. Women are more likely than men to leave their jobs because of a difficult manager. In one European study, women's satisfaction with their working life was significantly correlated with unsympathetic bosses and colleagues. Other sources of dissatisfaction are managers who don't listen, unclear performance objectives and lacking the appropriate resources to do the job. Where these work-related stressors exist, women are more likely than men to leave their organization.

Women are more likely than men to feel that they have to leave their organization in order to progress. In one study, more than half the senior women interviewed expressed their intention to leave the organization; within six months a staggering 25% had done so. They saw a lack of senior women as a lack of meritocracy in promotion and a lack of support for their development. The costs of such unnecessary departures are extremely high: substantial talent is lost, replacement costs are significant, and the cycle is perpetuated for women.

In US Fortune 1000 companies, most senior women who left their organization and joined a rival firm moved to CEO, CFO or EVP positions. Over 50% of these women had operations or legal/general counsel experience. The average education level of women in operational or legal/general counsel roles was well above the average for senior women in the sample and significantly higher than for women in HR, general administration or communication roles. These are the women who are in highest demand. They possess significant talent capital and are highly likely to be headhunted particularly where there is a perception of talent scarcity.

A recent Catalyst study declared that inequality remains entrenched and the pipeline at the top is not healthy, basing their conclusions on a study of US MBA graduates. Despite achieving parity in education, significant investment in diversity and inclusion programs, and women's acceleration into the workforce, the pipeline at the top was not filled with a balance of men and women equally supported and ready to move into top roles.

Attending to gender diversity issues will ensure that the best talent is retained. The most talented women must be inspired, nurtured and encouraged if the low numbers of women at executive levels are to change. Individualized career paths for high potential women that work on elastic time horizons have a greater chance of ensuring female high potentials are developed to their full capacity and retained to contribute to the success of the organisation.

Figure 11. Current position level of US MBAs who graduated between 1996 and 2007

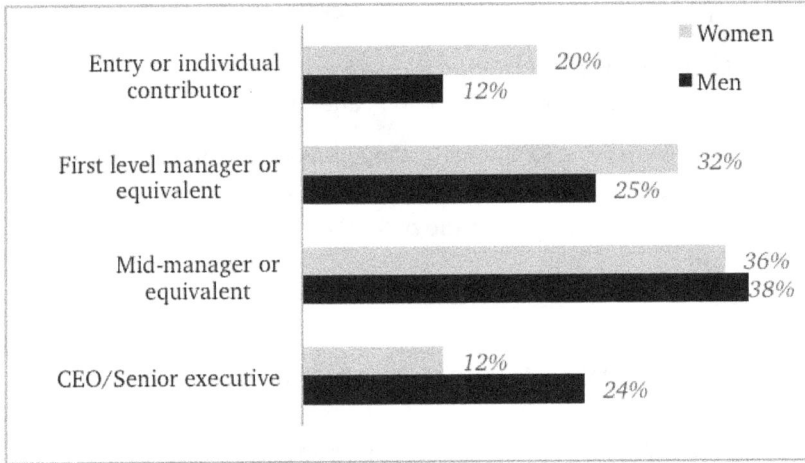

Where women feel unsuccessful at influencing masculine work cultures they are less likely to remain within the organization.

Most women who leave the organization due to career advancement barriers do so quietly, rather than drawing attention to the barriers or attempting to change discriminatory practices. This indicates that organizations need to be sensitively attuning women's experiences, and listen differently in order to understand how they might turnaround such departures.

Men are more likely overall to quit an organization. Both men and women quit more often for reasons other than family. The fact of women quitting their jobs to stay home and look after their children has been misperceived as women quitting more often than men.

Impediments to women's progress need to be surfaced and addressed if more women are to pledge to long-term commitment to the organization.

To do

✓ **Identify high risk women** (e.g., those in high profile assignments or male dominated environments) and pay particular attention to them, check in on a regular basis from HR, ensure they have manager/sponsor/mentor/coach support, connect them with the CEO.

✓ **Ensure all women leaving have an exit interview** and don't assume that women leave to look after their families.

✓ Follow up periodically with talented women who leave the organisation to know what they do and how they are developing their careers; **keep open the potential for talented women to return.**

5.5 RECOGNITION AND REWARD

Review 5.5: Assess your organization's progress: Are performance management and reward outcomes equally fair to both women and men?

✓✓✓ Our performance management and recognition systems have been thoroughly assessed and we have achieved recognition and salary equity

✓✓ The gender gaps in performance ratings and salaries have been identified and specific actions have been agreed to achieve parity

✓ Our policy and procedures instruct managers on how to avoid gender bias when assessing performance and reviewing salaries

✗ We trust the ability of managers to manage fairly and consider it unlikely that there are any equity issues

Cultural beliefs manifest themselves in two important areas of organizational life, deciding performance outcomes and awarding remuneration. There is no shortage of data demonstrating that women are assessed differently to men and that the substantial variation in salaries and incentives provided to men and women continues.

"You have to approach it in the same way that you would any issue in the organization.... You can't be more emotional about diversity You look at what's working, what's not working and you try different approaches and then you measure it. It's business. We lose the plot if we think that this is something different."
Alan Joyce, CEO, Qantas

For example, in Australia, women comprise 5% of top earners in ASX200 companies and 13% of top earners where there are two or more women on the board. Top female earners earn 58% of comparable male earners. In contrast, female executives earn 10 to 20% more and are nearly 20% more likely to be in the top five earners in organisations that have gender-diverse management than in those that are male-dominated.

5.5.1   Performance appraisal

A great deal of research highlights the significant impact that gender beliefs have on performance ratings and recognition of performance.

When a work environment is dominated by one gender, comparisons of performance tend to be in favour of the majority gender, regardless of whether it is male or female. Identically described and highly competent men and women are judged differently in male-dominated contexts. A number of research studies have shown that descriptions of the same behaviour when attributed to men are more highly rated than when attributed to women.

In male dominated environments standards of success are usually measured in male terms, making it more difficult for women to be judged as successful. In fact, in organizations that are male-dominated, women and men rate women less favourably in terms of success. Consequently, women have lower levels of job satisfaction, lower expectations and a reduced desire for promotion. Gender-linked expectations carry greater weight in the executive suite, where women are seen as less able than men to succeed.

Women's success is often attributed to external factors rather than the woman's own capabilities, and so women's contributions are diminished.

Women bosses are judged more harshly than men. Evaluations of women are lower overall than for men, especially when the leader's competence is evaluated, or when satisfaction with the leader is assessed.

Women are also held to stricter standards of promotion. Male and female executives know that gender comes into play when women's leadership is evaluated. When executives evaluate the leadership performance of male and female colleagues, they are 25 times more likely to comment on the woman's gender. Women executives may demonstrate all the behaviours for their current or more senior roles, yet they will still be identified for their gender: the same does not apply for men.

Awareness of these issues is the first step, but having the right skills, processes and systems is also necessary. Where there is a lack of structure in decision-making it is easier for stereotyped expectations to filter into performance assessment. There is often a concerted effort not to be rigid in performance assessments, particularly at senior levels, remaining open to uniqueness in managerial talent. The disadvantage of doing so is that gender expectations too easily filter into assessments.

Managers can minimize bias when they pay thoughtful attention to the filters they use and the expectations they have, and seek to apply a fairer lens to their performance appraisal of women and men. Ensuring the same amount of time is devoted to performance conversations, and using the same agenda for those conversations are small tactics that can help minimize bias.

Very few companies provide managers with training in how to avoid bias when evaluating the performance of others. Few companies have these checks and balances to guard against gender assumptions in performance review systems; competencies may be stereotypically masculine and evaluations may not be reviewed from a gender perspective.

Pepsico has established a number of mechanisms in its people processes that provide a robust framework by which managers can ensure fair performance reviews, with supporting checks and balances managed by the Human Resources function. The framework includes a partnership model of growth with shared responsibility for success, dual performance ratings and forced distribution based on results, detailed guidance regarding advancement, transparent accountability mechanisms particularly in relation to compensation and visible leadership of the process. HR regularly analyses the outcomes of performance reviews, checking parity.

People rarely intend to reproduce gender inequalities, yet persistent beliefs are prevalent and lead to their perpetuation.

If women are to gain their rightful place at senior levels of organizations, the biases that are endemic to performance appraisal practices must be rectified. To overcome the differential assessment of performance, it is recommended that the specificity of behaviours and outcomes required be increased and performance evaluations are monitored and challenged for gender bias.

To do

✓ Focus manager development on **awareness raising of differential career support for men and women,** awareness of subjective decision-making and how to avoid it, identify the benefits of having fuller talent available to them, train them in career management skills, help them identify how to promote the visibility of women.

✓ **Audit performance reviews from a gender perspective** and assess parity in ratings.

5.5.2   Fair remuneration

Not only are identically described men and women judged differently, they are also recognized and rewarded differently: the amount of recognition that women receive and the recommendations regarding their compensation are reliably lower than for men.

Women receive less recognition for their accomplishments. They receive fewer instances of recognition, the recognition they receive is more ambivalent and it is less predictable than the recognition that men receive. Women routinely underestimate their own abilities, while men have an inflated sense of their own: these estimates are accurate reflections of the amount of praise women and men receive, but they are not accurate reflections of achievements or abilities. This lack of recognition is one factor affecting women's career goals and the level of effort they are willing to put into pursuing them and it is a key reason why women abandon their ambitions.

Women overall in Australia earn 18% less than male peers in similar positions. In Australia female graduates are paid on average $3,000 less than male graduates in their first jobs and in the US female MBA graduates are paid $US5,600 less than their male counterparts. At middle management, the disparity increases to 25% less and amongst high performers at the most senior levels, women earn only 58% of what comparable top males earn, indicating a significant disparity. US female CEOs earn 67% of male CEOs and female CFOs earn 59% of their male counterparts. Over a working lifetime it is estimated that a woman working the same job for the same time will earn on average $A1million less than a man.

Detailed analysis of the gender wage gap in Australia by NATSEM has demonstrated that discrimination plays a significant role. Financial modelling demonstrates that firm size (a higher proportion of women work in smaller firms) accounts for 3%, vocational qualifications (women have fewer) accounts for 5%, time in the workforce and tenure (women have lower) accounts for 7% and industry segregation (predominately male occupations pay more than predominately female) accounts for 25%

of the differential between male and female remuneration. At 60%, by far the largest contributor to the wage differential is being a woman.

Figure 12. Factors contributing to the gender wage gap

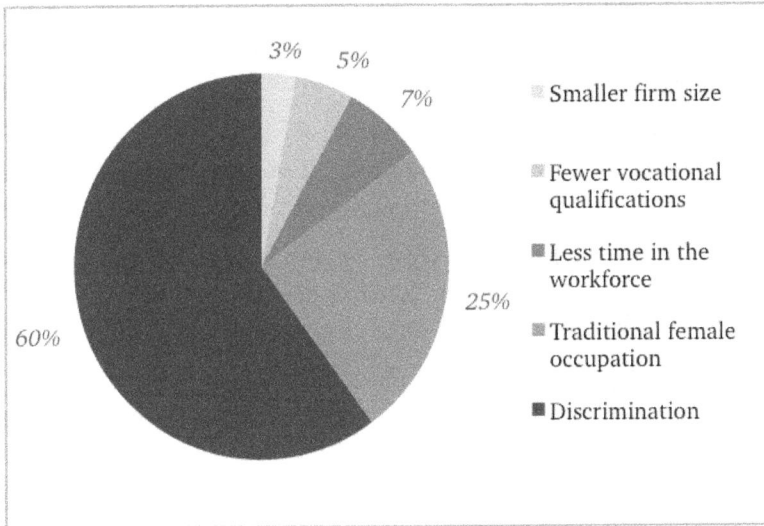

Women comprise 13% of top earners when there are two or more women on the board, and appear among the top corporate earners where this is the case. This shift in overall remuneration profile highlights the impact of bias and reinforces the importance of fair organizational remuneration practices that are monitored and reported, and then actively managed.

About one third of Australian companies report that they review salaries to reduce gaps between men's and women's pay. Swinburne University of Technology developed a University Pay Equity Strategy 2008-2012 to bridge the gap between male and female remuneration.

Equal opportunity legislation was designed some time ago to effect equal pay. Clearly legislation is not enough. Organizations that want gender balanced leadership need to ensure equal pay for men and women in equal roles.

Salary differentials can partly be understood by knowing that women approach their remuneration rather differently to men. Women are more likely to define career success in terms of intrinsic rewards such as personal achievements, professional development and achievement of work-life balance. On the other hand, men are more likely to define career success in terms of higher salaries, promotion and achievement of status symbols. Whether or not women and men consider their remuneration is fair for their role will therefore be judged through a more complex lens than just extrinsic rewards like pay.

Because of women's different perspective regarding remuneration, they are less demanding than men in salary discussions. Individual discussions with women regarding their remuneration may reinforce these differences.

Men are much more likely than women to negotiate over a salary offer for a new role. This pattern is likely to continue with each new role, and at each review. The disadvantage for women is in more than salary, and extends to visibility, training and career growth.

Women are more likely to seek conciliation through negotiation whereas men are more likely to approach negotiation in a competitive manner. As a consequence, women demand and accept less than men in salary negotiations, and are less satisfied with the way they negotiate. They are less likely to initiate negotiations, view negotiation more negatively, are less confident and set lower goals. Women do not feel the same entitlement to higher salaries as men.

In addition, women are seen negatively when they ask for more money, reflecting as it does a schema of self-interest: this same perception does not apply to men who ask for more money as they can legitimately project self-interest. When women advocate for others, rather than themselves, it is generally more acceptable as it fits the prevailing schema of women: in fact, women's performance ratings increase where they negotiate on behalf of others.

Women should have as much opportunity to negotiate their remuneration as men, yet the gender imbalance in negotiating preferences contributes to significant differences in remuneration as well as advancement. The nature of the opportunity extends from awareness and use of negotiation as an option, the amount of time given in which to conduct negotiations, and the final negotiation outcome.

Some organizations may consider this an opportunity to reinforce the current pay differentials: best practice organizations are concerned to provide a level playing field for both genders, and ensure that remuneration is determined on the basis of performance and capability, rather than 'you get what you ask for'. Best practice organizations hold managers accountable for equal remuneration, provide transparent advice and information to women about remuneration, monitor practices, adjust discrepancies when they occur, and ensure a system that doesn't favour one gender over the other. Women and men can therefore be equally remunerated for their equal capabilities and performance.

Making remuneration information public has the potential to undo some of the largest gender effects, providing visibility and transparency of remuneration practices. Managers and organizations vigilant to the different negotiating styles of men and women avoid discrimination by noticing who asks for what, when and how often, and providing a fair balance of opportunities and outcomes to men and women based on competence and performance.

To do

✓ **Ensure managers are aware of women's propensity to attribute successes to others and men's to themselves,** rebalance the amount of praise given so that it is commensurate with abilities, increase the recognition given to women for their performance.

✓ **Provide transparent advice** and information to women about remuneration and negotiation of remuneration.

✓ Provide management training in **how to negotiate** with men and women.

✓ Publish remuneration information and **provide transparent information about how remuneration is decided** and reviewed.

✓ **Audit salary increases and bonuses** prior to final decisions and recalibrate to achieve parity.

✓ **Develop a plan for equity in remuneration.**

Checklist of Fair talent and performance management actions

Identify the extent to which your organization has implemented the following actions, using the rating system:

1. We already do this well

2. In train, with room for improvement

3. We don't do this, or do it poorly

Fair talent and performance management actions	Rating
5.1 Talent identification	
5.1.1 Identifying potential • Audit and adjust leadership competencies to be gender neutral. • Review talent guidelines and raise awareness of the possibility of subtle bias and institute audits to ensure gender-free talent reviews. • Ensure equal gender targets in succession and high potential programs. Ensure these talent processes are open to scrutiny and that decision-making has clear criteria. • Support women as they join the succession pool. • When high potential women miss out on promotions, conduct an objective review of processes and outcomes and provide them with comprehensive feedback for development and support to close gaps.	
5.1.2 Leadership potential • Assess the organisation's definition of leadership and review the competency model to avoid a masculine depiction of leadership and instead offer a wide range of leadership capabilities and styles. • As part of leadership development programs, highlight responsibility for gender equity and the value of diversity.	

Fair talent and performance management actions	Rating
5.1.3 Barriers removed • Provide or advocate for training for managers in awareness and impact of bias, recognising the different behaviours of men and women, having career conversations, and thinking creatively about ways to engage women in their careers while balancing family responsibilities.	
5.1.4 Same rate of progress • At or around age 30, do a career review for all managerial, professional and high potential women, providing expert career advice and the opportunity to discuss career aspirations and opportunities. • Ensure that key roles have either been undertaken or are planned, to provide breadth in knowledge and experience. • Discuss family aspirations and identify the barriers that might be encountered and how they could be overcome to maximise career success. • Assess the level of support that has been provided by line managers and intervene in relationships that do not seem to be benefiting women. Avoid biases in selection for promotion: make progression rates transparent.	

Fair talent and performance management actions	Rating
5.2 Recruitment and selection	
• Review recruitment and talent policies to alert managers to communication and negotiation style differences. Consider reporting mechanisms for managers who fail to promote a targeted percentage of women. • Promote the CEO's involvement in all senior recruitment activities, driving a deeper pool of female candidates, not accepting less than equity, and not accepting the first candidate pool provided if that is not equitable. • Audit job descriptions and job advertisements for bias and image. • Increase awareness of the subtle impact of biases, put measures in place to avoid easy hiring decisions and use creative options for increasing the pool of female candidates. • Create transparent monitoring of numbers of women at each recruitment decision point. • Increase the attractiveness of certain line roles, e.g. by clustering women together to create a critical mass rather than distributing them thinly, which creates a barrier to women's participation.	
5.3 Development	
5.3.1 Sponsor support • Sponsor high potential women. • Provide and undertake training in high quality mentorship.	

Fair talent and performance management actions	Rating
5.3.2 Fair access to high profile assignments • Prime women to understand and request developmental aspects in their job roles. • Audit and monitor the distribution of high profile assignments across gender. • Support a CEO forum for women in line management roles to discuss business/operational issues, provide direct access to the CEO and other senior organisational champions. • Encourage senior organisation leaders to invite women into their key networks ensuring they are fully integrated into power groups. • Provide networking opportunities during working hours, ensure high potential women are members of and develop influential networks, facilitate introductions and build confidence. Prime women to understand and request developmental aspects in their job roles.	
5.3.3 Gender specific programs • Provide a range of gender-specific programs. • Provide networking/skills development programs for younger women to introduce them to the leadership domain and build their confidence and ambition as future leaders. • Provide women's only development programs and networks for middle and senior women to develop strategies for being a part of the dominant paradigm.	

Fair talent and performance management actions	Rating
5.4 Retention	
• Identify high risk women (e.g., those in high profile assignments or male dominated environments) and pay particular attention to them, check in on a regular basis from HR, ensure they have manager/sponsor/ mentor/coach support, connect them with the CEO. • Ensure all women leaving have an exit interview and don't assume that women leave to look after their families. • Follow up periodically with talented women who leave the organisation to know what they do and how they are developing their careers; keep open the potential for talented women to return.	
5.5 Recognition and reward	
5.5.1 Performance appraisal	
• Focus manager development on awareness raising of differential career support for men and women, awareness of subjective decision-making and how to avoid it, identify the benefits of having fuller talent available to them, train them in career management skills, help them identify how to promote the visibility of women. • Audit performance reviews from a gender perspective and assess parity in ratings.	
5.5.2 Fair remuneration	
• Ensure managers are aware of women's propensity to attribute successes to others and men's to themselves, rebalance the amount of praise given so that it is commensurate with abilities, increase the recognition given to women for their performance. • Provide transparent advice and information to women about remuneration and negotiation of remuneration. • Provide management training in how to negotiate with men and women and get fair outcomes. • Publish remuneration information and provide transparent information about how remuneration is decided and reviewed. • Audit salary increases and bonuses prior to final decisions and recalibrate to achieve parity.	

What are three key actions that would help progress Fair talent and performance management in your organisation?

1. _____

2. _____

3. _____

6.

TAKING ACTION

"Programs are the first stage in making a difference. Managers being accountable for the diversity of their teams and eliminating behaviour that is unacceptable is the next stage of driving cultural change."
~ Stephen Fitzgerald, former Chairman,
Goldman Sachs A&NZ

Everyone can make a contribution to the achievement of gender balance in senior leadership. The preceding chapters identified a series of actions that can be taken according to your organization's gender diversity status. This chapter augments that by helping you design your own personal awareness and development program. It shows you how you can become more aware of unconscious associations you hold that can unknowingly bias your behavior, create better congruence between your conscious and unconscious beliefs, and identify how to make better decisions.

6.1 ASSESSING YOUR UNCONSCIOUS BELIEFS

Just how big a role gender plays in shaping our identity and decisions is only now being realized. Gender dynamics tend to occur below the surface, and outside of conscious awareness. Not only that, but some of what's happening below the surface contradicts what's happening at the surface level. The ability to tap into our unconscious might sound unlikely, but has been the subject of increasingly sophisticated research: by completing the following exercises you can gain closer insight into your unconscious gender beliefs.

"It's about the legacy you leave and diversity is a key part of that. ..... If I do it right, Qantas will be much more rounded, more representative for a national icon and much stronger for the next 90 years. If I leave with the right diversity in place, then it's a job well done."
Alan Joyce, CEO, Qantas

There is no intention to inculcate a particular set of beliefs as being better than others. Yes, there is an emphasis on change, because many people find that their unconscious beliefs are not what they want them to be. If that's the case for you, the chapter provides information on how to be clearer about the factors that influence your decisions and make better informed choices.

6.1.1 Understanding unconscious associations

As discussed in Chapter 3, we have a parallel system of conscious and unconscious beliefs that guide our actions.

These impact in many domains, not just diversity. Management decisions are impacted by a vast array of these biases, which help us make decisions quickly, but may lead to decisions of lesser quality. Decisions are affected by our self-interest, dissenting views may not be adequately explored, we may be overly influenced by a past success or we may be loss averse. (For further information on decision biases read Kahneman, Lovallo & Siboney).

Our cognitive processing is subject to many distortions, such as demonstrated by the diagram on the left.
http://visiontestgame.com/funny-easy-easy- optical-illusions-to-draw-for-kids/

While there are two distinct images, it can be difficult to see all of the information at once. We generally focus on one rather than the other and can have some difficulty identifying the second image. The image seen first varies from person to person. Once the two images are pointed out, the distortion becomes very obvious.

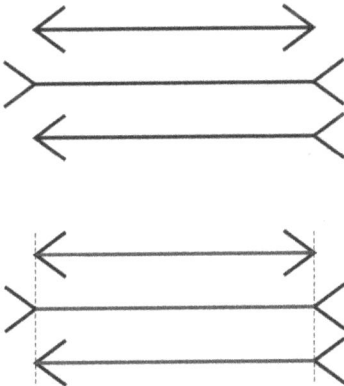

Likewise, the directions of the arrows at the end of lines in the adjacent diagram distort our perception of the length of the lines, giving the appearance that the lines have different lengths when in fact they are of equal length.
http://en.wikipedia.org/wiki/Müller-Lyer_illusion

Now consider whether the two tables in the following diagram are the same size and shape or whether they are different.

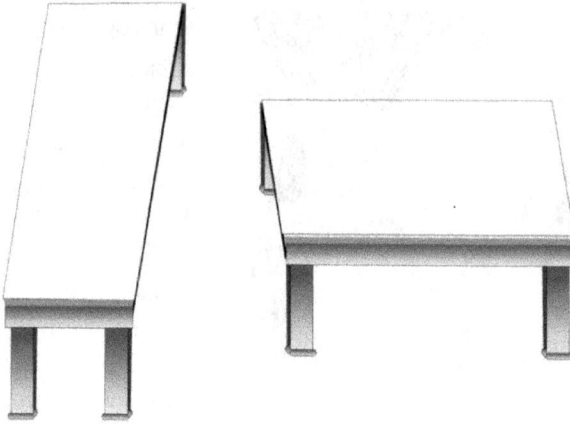

While the tables have the appearance of being different, they are in fact the same size and shape.

Seeing the tables from different angles changes the perspective and distorts the way we see them. Distortions in decision-making about people operate in a similar manner.

Consider the following list of traits:

- Empathy
- Understanding
- Gentle
- Focus on the needs of others
- Kind
- Soft

- Expressive
- Fearful
- Wonderful
- Weak
- Sentimental
- Submissive

Is this a list of traits that describe men?

This list of traits is commonly associated with women, not men. The traits are known as communal traits and are easily recognizable as such. This association has a high degree of consensus and credibility in our society.

Similarly, consider this second list of traits:

- Focus on own needs
- Task oriented
- Tough
- Competitive
- Assertive
- Competent

- Ambitious
- Bad but bold
- Adventurous
- Dominant
- Forceful
- Independent

This vastly different list of traits, labelled agentic traits, is commonly associated with men.

The association of particular traits with gender, our gender schema, is well learnt from an early age and generally unconsciously held, even where we no longer consciously agree with it.

Both sets of traits are desirable, but in different ways. Men, as agentic, are respected, while women, as communal, are liked, reinforcing differential power attributions. Men are associated with power therefore with authority and status while women are associated with nurturing, lower status, and support positions.

These associations are typically so well learned that we don't have to think to make the right connection between the list of traits and the gender. Section 3.1.3 Bias acknowledged explains more about these traits and conscious and unconscious associations.

6.1.2   Assessing unconscious associations

You can test your own unconscious beliefs about gender, at a Harvard University demonstration site. The test takes 10 to 15 minutes. Instructions appear on the following page.

> Go to the **HARVARD IMPLICIT PROJECT** website:
> https://implicit.harvard.edu/implicit/
>
> Click on: "SOCIAL ATTITUDES" & continue as a Guest
>
> Click on: "TAKE A TEST" on the top menu bar
>
> Click on: "I WISH TO PROCEED"
>
> Click on: You may also later choose to complete Gender-Science IAT or any of the other categories that interest you.
>
> Click on: "CLICK HERE TO BEGIN"

Complete the test. *Make a note of your results,* and how they compare with the large sample comparison group: your results will appear on the page but they won't be saved for you to return to later.

The chart on the following page shows the results for 83,084 test takers and their unconscious associations between male and female, and family and career.

Black bars represent stronger associations of female with family and male with career. They account for 76% of the sample (20% have a slight association, 32% a moderate association and 24% a strong association).

White bars represent little or no association and represent 17% of the total sample. Finally, grey bars represent stronger associations of male with family and female with career which is the case for 6% of respondents.

The results demonstrate how widely held these automatic associations are. How do your results compare?

Automatic associations and bias are **not** the same thing, but having the associations can lead to bias. As unconscious associations are so well learned, they become automatic and then unconscious: they sit at the heart of bias.

Figure 13. IAT gender and work associations

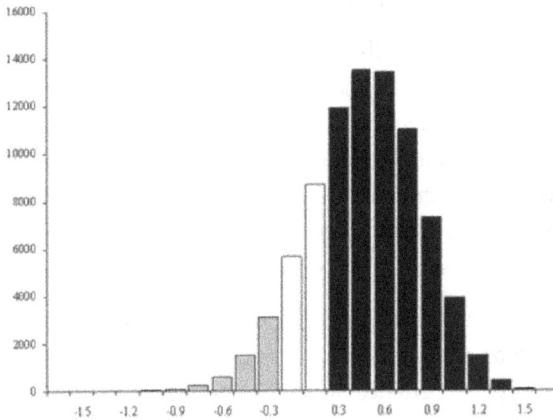

Many people are surprised or even confronted by their test results, if they differ from their conscious beliefs. It is important to understand that it is common for this disparity to occur.

Being aware of the difference between conscious and unconscious beliefs is an important step in minimizing the possibility of any bias, so don't be concerned. Many people are motivated by their test results to close the gap between their unconscious and their conscious beliefs. The following section provides assistance on how you can do this.

As already discussed, people hold conscious as well as unconscious beliefs. If you are interested in further assessment of your conscious gender associations, go to Peter Glick's website and take the Ambivalent Sexism Inventory:

http://www.understandingprejudice.org/asi/

You'll also find on the website a brief summary of the research behind the measure and an explanation of what the results mean.

6.1.3   Gender identity

Gender is a concept we learn early and thoroughly and it is claimed to be the most powerful feature of our identity. It's an important part of negotiating who we are and how we navigate the world. The following exercise assists you to develop a deeper understanding of how your own gender beliefs were developed and have shaped your identity.

Think about the messages that you have received about being male or being female and what was and wasn't acceptable for you to do and be. What impact did they have on you and the important people in your life? Consider each of the following key contexts that inform the development of identity and list the critical influences on you in each of these contexts. What lessons did you learn about gender and your gendered self? How did these shape your sense of who you are?

A conscious exploration of identity helps you understand patterns you have developed as a leader, conflicts you habitually experience, successes and challenges you experience. In particular, it helps understand how you developed the unconscious associations you identified in Section 6.1.2 above.

Family background	What key messages do you carry with you from childhood? Family is our first organization and our parents and other close family members provide our first experiences of leadership and authority. What gender roles did your parents enact? Birth order can be formative and establish enduring patterns, e.g., oldest daughter or son. What key gender lessons did you learn in your family? How have they shaped your development as a leader?
Social/ cultural background	What key messages do you live out based on important social or cultural patterns to which you have been exposed? What expectations did the society you were brought up in have about what it meant to be male or female? What happened to people who behaved outside of these expectations and how did that impact you? How have these expectations changed over time and what difference has it made to you?

Professional socialization	How was your sense of self and engagement with the world formed through your development as a professional? How did/does gender feature in your professional training and development? Are you in a male or female-dominated or neutral profession or role? How important is this to you, what impact does it have on your sense of your self?
Organization context	How do your organization's expectations and culture shape your sense of who you are? What kinds of experiences are different if you are a man or a woman? What is possible or not possible based on your gender?
Crucibles and crises	These are the big changes in life. Significant shifts in geography, language, socioeconomic status, etc. can be tipping points in our lives. Such crises cause us to question and reshape our identity. How have these experiences influenced the way you see yourself, your gender, and the world?
Other key experiences	Are there other kinds of experiences that have shaped your gender identity?

6.2 IDENTIFYING WHAT TO DO

"It was deeply satisfying. Fifteen of the eighteen senior women attending have had real breakthroughs since then. Many have said my attendance helped. It also allowed me to get in touch with, and to some extent, remove, barriers. It also sent a message about just how important elevating women's leadership is to me."
Andrew Stevens, former CEO, IBM A&NZ

6.2.1 Overview of what can be done
Unconscious beliefs are difficult to change. They are overlearned and habitual, and exist outside our conscious awareness and it is these features

that make them difficult to change. Nevertheless there are some strategies that can decrease them and minimize bias.

Reducing the likelihood of unconscious bias can be achieved through:

- Understanding what unconscious bias is and how it works (see Sections 3.3 Bias acknowledged and 3.4 Backlash managed)

- Becoming aware of the unconscious beliefs we hold and how they may affect decisions (see Section 6.1.2 Assessing your own unconscious bias, above)

- Recognizing that unconscious beliefs may be quite different from our espoused beliefs – when people discover that their unconscious beliefs are contradictory to their espoused egalitarian views, they can be highly motivated to change and become particularly aware of their behaviour in group settings (see Section 6.1.2 Assessing your own unconscious bias, above and Chapter 3)

- Taking a public, moral stance on the issue of gender equality (see Section 2.2 Leadership Commitment)

- Developing exposure to and relationships with admirable gender exemplars (See Sections 2.2.3 Senior executive role models and champions and 5.3 Sponsor support for development)

- Engaging in counter-stereotypical activities, recognizing and highlighting success at counter-stereotypical activities

- Ensuring a context in which bias can be controlled, for example, making considered decisions rather than decisions on the fly, and focusing on congruence between nonverbal and verbal behaviour (see Section 6.2.2 A Framework to minimize bias, below)

- Increasing the transparency of decision processes and outcomes (see Section 6.2.2 A Framework to minimize bias, below)

- Changing the automatic gender associations we have by practicing different associations, such as woman strong, and man warm

Changing unconscious beliefs is relatively difficult – we're dealing with patterns of thought that we've had for all of our lives and that we haven't necessarily been aware of. Trying to change unconscious beliefs does not always appear to work and research shows that some attempts can backfire. Being forced to engage in training or awareness of unconscious bias can strengthen bias as can attempting to suppress it.

6.2.2 A Framework to minimize bias

Figure 14. Framework to minimize bias

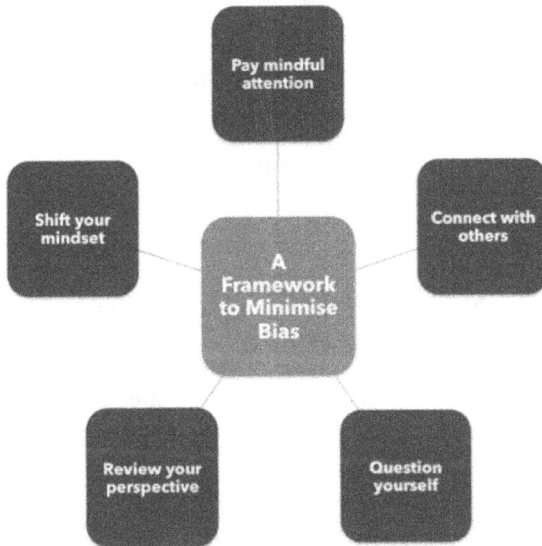

1. *Pay mindful attention*

Better managing your attention can help you to disconnect from automatic associations and responses.

Attention is the currency of leadership and how you direct and sustain your attention is critical. Mindfulness techniques are particularly effective in helping you manage your attention more effectively. Mindfulness involves training the mind to pay attention in a particular way. It is the nonjudgmental observation of the ongoing stream of internal and external stimuli.

Mindfulness involves consciously bringing awareness to here-and-now experience with openness, interest, and receptiveness. Jon Kabat-Zinn, a world authority on the use of mindfulness training, defines it as: 'Paying attention in a particular way: on purpose, in the present moment, and non-judgmentally.' Many similar definitions exist, including that of Russ Harris: 'Consciously bringing awareness to your here-and-now experience, with openness, interest and receptiveness.'

There are many different mindfulness techniques, all of which are designed to increase three things:

- Paying attention to the present moment through the careful observation of all perceptions, thoughts, emotions, or sensations
- The non-judgmental acceptance of all thoughts, feelings and experiences
- Managing the focus of your attention with ease and flexibility.

Unconscious associations are most likely to impact decisions when:

- Decision criteria aren't clear
- There isn't time, or we don't take the time, to deliberate over the decision
- Information is ambiguous
- They are not subject to scrutiny.

Instances where we are making decisions quickly and intuitively are most likely to be affected by unconscious associations. On the other hand, when we take the opportunity to deliberate over decisions and consider a wide variety of possible options, weighing the costs and benefits of each, we minimize the impact of unconscious associations.

Mindfulness techniques provide a simple and effective means to interrupt our reliance on automatic thoughts.

The following STOP activity is a very simple, brief mindfulness technique that may be instituted at moments of decision. It is a technique to decouple decisions from automatic responses that may bias our decisions.

S top and interrupt your 'automatic pilot' by concentrating on the present moment

T ake a breath and bring your focus to the experience of the in-breath and the out-breath.

O pen to observation. Connect to the experience of this moment and inquire with a sense of curiosity:

– What am I seeing, feeling, sensing, hearing, smelling, thinking?

P roceed and reconnect with your surroundings and with your activity in the moment.

(Adapted from Openground Mindfulness Based Stress Reduction training manual.)

The STOP technique helps disrupt the pattern. Having disrupted the pattern, what next? Manage your attention by shifting the focus of your attention to those you are with, particularly if they are a different gender, cultural or racial group. Seek to understand their perceptions and experiences.

2.   *Connect with others*

There are many different ways of paying attention to information. Often, the focus is on getting the task done. The second step in the framework is to focus greater attention on others around you, emphasizing personal relationship rather than task orientation.

A useful tool for doing this is based on perceptual positions, which represent perspectives on the world. Each position provides a different perspective:

a)   In first position (I) your attention is focused on your own subjective experience

b)   In second position (You) your attention is focused on how another person views the world (including how they view you)

c)   In third position (We) your attention is focused on neutral observation.

In first position, you experience the world through your own eyes. First position focuses your attention on your inner experience, how you are thinking and feeling about your ideas and experiences. From first position, you develop a sense of self. First position is one of advocacy.

First position relies on language that refers things back to you, e.g., 'I feel ....', 'I think ....', 'My opinion about that is ...', 'You are wrong about that ...', 'What I would do in that situation is ...'.

Operating predominately from first position restricts the ability to form relationships as you are aware of what matters to you to the exclusion of other information. Being primarily in first position reduces your ability to understand others; you have your own distorted perceptions of another on which you base your engagement, which may or may not be accurate.

Someone stuck in first position is generally seen as egotistical, self-centred and insensitive.

Second position is essential in building and maintaining relationships. It represents empathy, 'putting yourself in another's shoes', if you check carefully that your assumptions about what the person is thinking and feeling are accurate. From second position, you understand how someone else experiences the world and how they experience you. Second position is one of inquiry.

From second position you use language that refers things to the other person, e.g., 'I notice you are ...', 'I hear you say ...', 'That seems to suggest you are ...', 'I don't know if this is right, but you seem ...'.

Operating predominately in second position means that you spend too much time paying attention to others and lose yourself. Someone stuck in second position is generally seen as a caretaker or rescuer.

By operating in second position when working with people who have a different background and experience set to your own, you can prevent a reliance on stereotypes and rules about the group called women and instead focus on the individual characteristics of this particular person.

From third position you experience the situation as an external, neutral observer whether or not you are a participant in it. You watch what happens and understand it without experiencing the direct emotions of those involved (including yourself).

In third position you use language that is impersonal, such as 'It seems that …', 'We might assume …', 'People sometimes …'.

Operating predominately in third position means that you develop only superficial relationships and lose your own sense of self. Someone stuck in third position is generally seen as detached, impersonal and cold.

Third position allows you to monitor your interactions with people who are different to you, assessing the level of engagement and openness.

Consider the following example.

If someone requests flexible working arrangements and you respond with your attention in first position, you will be absorbed by your own emotions and needs. You may focus on your concern for resourcing and the impact on workloads and time-frames. You may be particularly busy and the request means having to add another problem onto your list of things to do. Alternatively, you may identify ways in which the use of flexible working arrangements would be particularly beneficial, but the perspective here is your own, rather than the other person's. First position is generally the least helpful position to rely on when managing relational situations.

If you respond in second position then you are likely to notice the needs and interests of the person making the request and be able to engage with the issue from their perspective. You might respond by empathizing with their needs, and asking how their needs might best be met while ensuring work outcomes are achieved.

If you respond in third position, you are likely to identify the corporate policies that apply and how they are relevant in this instance, explore examples of other situations where people have undertaken flexible working arrangements and what the result was. You might ask the person what impact different arrangements might have on others and how they might be minimized if negative, and maximized if positive.

Overall, attention is divided into the three positions; being aware of how you control your attention allows you to organize it more deliberately to get the outcomes you seek. Do a quick self-assessment. How much time do you spend in each of the three modes, on average? Which mode is most comfortable to you? How easy or difficult is it to adopt second position with people who are different from you? If/when people who are different from you make requests, how do you respond to them?

If you work with people as a manager the general rule is that first position should receive the least amount of your attention, about 15%, as less awareness is needed on the self. About half of your attention is focused in second position, allowing you to monitor the people with whom you relate and to deal with issues as they arise. About 35% of your attention is in third position which allows you to maintain perspective on the interactions around you, to manage ideas and information, and to manage the situation.

3.   *Question yourself*

Pausing, opening up to others' perspectives and then questioning yourself, help prevent automatic thinking and the potential for biases to guide your decision.

Rather than presuming you know the right answer or approach to a problem or decision, take a step back and question your motives, needs and interpretation of the situation, even where it is highly familiar and you believe you have all the capability you need to act.

Rather than moving immediately to action or advocating your own position, take a learning orientation by opening up the conversation using questions that seek further information, exploring other viewpoints and clarifying your own and others' positions. What are your blind spots or gaps in knowledge that might alter your interpretation of the best course of action to take?

Remain open to new perspectives and ideas:

- Survey a wide range of objectives

- Assess all relevant values

- Canvass alternative courses of action and assess their advantages and disadvantages

- Deliberately seek new information including data that counters your viewpoint

- Avoid a too-rapid conclusion to the decision-making process

- Ensure there is ample time to implement decisions

- Review and adjust the impact of decisions.

4.   *Review your perspective*

Questioning yourself can occur in the decision-making moment and can also occur through reflection. Reflection is a good way to get a broader perspective on your approach and your decision-making. Colleagues, mentors and coaches who are prepared to help challenge your thinking, rather than those who will reinforce your point of view, provide great support for opening up your decision-making to greater scrutiny and achieving a fairer perspective.

Identify one or two people with whom you can meet on a regular basis to help you explore new perspectives, develop a broader frame of reference and support your change process.

5.   *Shift your mindset*

Attuning people to their own biases builds awareness and starts a change process. Mindful attention to the likelihood of bias in a range of situations, such as selection and development, and making use of deliberative decision processes sets up the opportunity to minimize unconscious bias.

The fundamental question is 'what can I change?'

The preceding chapters of this book come with lists of actions. Some of these actions may already be part of your approach, whereas others are suggestions for what you can do.

6.2.3   Goal setting

Having goals is helpful because they shape the direction of action, influence the degree of effort exerted and increase the level of persistence of effort over time. Level of self-efficacy influences perceptions of the ability to achieve goals particularly when combined with their level of complexity: the greater the self-belief, the more difficult goals can be and the higher the level of performance as a result. Goals are least effective on complex tasks where there is no prior experience and high pressure to perform well, immediately.

What we know about goal setting:

1. **Commitment counts**: high commitment to goals results from believing the goal is both important and attainable. Making goals public demonstrates commitment and increases perceptions of accountability for and likelihood of effort being expended in achieving the goal. The more difficult the goal is to achieve, the greater the commitment needs to be.

2. **Clarity matters**: articulating goals specifically and clearly identifies the target of change and assists monitoring and accountability.

3. **Feedback** helps: Feedback that shows progress increases the likelihood of goal achievement. Regular feedback, on a daily basis, helps maintain momentum.

4. **Using the SMART** (Specific, Measurable, Achievable, Realistic and Time-bound) acronym to guide goal setting is an easy way to cover the important features of good goal setting.

> *"For me, this is all about, how we build great leaders. It's a broader shift. How do people lead other people? How do you work with each individual to make them successful? How do you create an environment which is inclusive, where everyone can perform to their potential? That's why this is so important."*
> David Thodey, CEO, Telstra

Chapters 2 to 5 identify actions you can take to progress your understanding of gender diversity and its benefits and the steps you can take to improve your organization's implementation of its gender diversity program. At the end of each chapter there is a checklist designed to assist you to identify actions that you can take in areas that are least well developed in yourself and your organization.

Choose two to three of those areas and develop goals that you will focus on for the next six months. You may already have a preferred format for goal setting, but if not, the following structure may assist.

Key areas to make sure you cover off on are:

- What actions must be taken to achieve the goal?
- Who is accountable for those actions?
- What are the timeframes for those actions?
- What barriers need to be overcome?
- What resources do you need?
- What must you give up in order to achieve the goal?
- What are the benefits of achieving the goal?

Two examples follow.

GOAL STATEMENT 1: Create a clear statement of the specific benefits that a better gender balance will achieve for my division and communicat it to all staff at our next leadership offsite (date). (Based on 2.1 Purpose)

WHAT MUST BE DONE TO ACHIEVE THE GOAL?

Translate some of the research indicators into meaningful numbers for my division, eg what would a 34% increase in profits as a percentage of revenue mean? Use our female consumer data and extrapolate to increased sales on the basis of better connections – what could we target in terms of increased sales

WHAT RESOURCES DO YOU NEED?

Finance manager and marketing manager to assist with the data. I will prepare th statement with assistance from Communications.

WHAT ARE THE TIMEFRAMES FOR THOSE ACTIVITIES?

Data to be produced by (date), first draft statement to be produced by (date).

WHAT BARRIERS NEED TO BE OVERCOME?

Challenges of time, identifying meaningful projections

WHAT MUST YOU GIVE UP IN ORDER TO ACHIEVE THE GOAL?

Some time on the leadership offsite agenda that might have been spent on other issues.

WHAT ARE THE BENEFITS OF ACHIEVING THE GOAL?

A compelling statement and good reasons for supporting the gender diversity program that are easy for me to communicate and share in various forums.

GOAL STATEMENT 2: Understand what unconscious bias is and how it affects the decisions I make, within 6 months. (Based on 3.3 Bias acknowledged.)

WHAT MUST BE DONE TO ACHIEVE THE GOAL?

Identify the training that is available, schedule it in my diary and participate.

WHAT RESOURCES DO YOU NEED?

Some expert advice on what training/coaching exists and where to access it. I will ask for feedback from my Senior manager Jane.

WHAT ARE THE TIMEFRAMES FOR THOSE ACTIVITIES?

Speak with HR by end of next fortnight (date).

WHAT BARRIERS NEED TO BE OVERCOME?

Challenges of time, not knowing what resources will work best for me.

WHAT MUST YOU GIVE UP IN ORDER TO ACHIEVE THE GOAL?

Some time, perhaps some certainty about how good my decision-making is!

WHAT ARE THE BENEFITS OF ACHIEVING THE GOAL?

I will be much better informed. I'll have some clues about what bias is and how I can engage better. Hopefully it will lead to some better decisions and increase the engagement of my female (and male?) staff.

6.2.4   Goal achievement

People are most motivated to put effort into learning where they can see progress. A daily checklist, and support from key people, helps keep attention focused on what needs to be done and what progress is being achieved.

Daily checklist of action

Based on your goals, develop a checklist for review at the end of each day. The checklist can be reviewed in five to ten minutes at the end of each working day and primes you to keep your goals in mind, enables you to notice your daily progress and allows you to fine-tune what you need to do tomorrow to make further progress.

The follow list provides an example of what your checklist might be like:

1. Did I pay attention differently today?

    *   Did I stop and and disconnect from my automatic thinking?

    *   What happened if and when I did?

    *   Did I spend more or less time with men and women? What was the quality of my interaction with each gender?

2. How much time did I spend in 2nd position, as opposed to 1st?

    *   Who did I connect with and build interpersonal relationship rather than just push forward on the task? Was this the same for men and women?

3. Did I question myself today?

4. Have I broadened my perspective today? What do I know or understand today that I didn't yesterday?

    *   Who helped me to do that?

5. What did I do differently today?

6. What progress did I make on my goals?

7. What's the one thing that I could do tomorrow that would best facilitate my progress?

Identify key people, such as colleagues, mentors, or your coach to provide support to you. Share your goals with them and ask them to provide you with feedback. Give them permission to challenge you. Make regular connections with them to obtain feedback on your progress.

As your goals are achieved, go back to the action checklists at the end of each chapter and select a replacement goal.

7.

SELECTED REFERENCES

Adler, R (undated). "Women in the executive suite correlate to high profits." European Project on Equal Pay" Downloaded from http://www. csripraktiken.se/wp-content/uploads/adler_web.pdf.24-11-10

Agars, MD (2004) "Reconsidering the impact of gender stereotypes on the advancement of women in organizations", Psychology of Women Quarterly, 28, 103-111.

Asgari, S., Dasgupta, N., & Cote, N.G. (2010). "When does contact with successful in-group members change self-stereotypes?", Social Psychology, 41(3), 203-211.

Babcock, L. & Laschever, S. (2009). "The costs of not negotiating", Harvard Business Review, January, Accessed at blogs.hbr.org/hmu/2009/01/is-talent-going-to-waste-in-yo.htm.

Becker, J.C. (2010). "Why do women endorse hostile and benevolent sexism? The role of salient female subtypes and internalization of sexist contents", Sex Roles, 62, 453- 467.

Bell, L.A. (2005). Women-led firms and the gender gap in top executive jobs, IZA DP No. 1689. Downloaded from http://papers.ssrn.com/sol3/papers.cfm?abstract_id=773964

Braund, C. & Medd, R. (2008). "WOB Road Map for Gender Diversity on Australian Boards", Women on Boards, October 2008.

Brown, D.A.H. Brown, D.L., & Anastasopoulos, V. (2002). "Women on Boards: Not just the right thing but the bright thing." The Conference Board, Canada.

Burke, R. J., & McKeen, C. A. (1996). Do women at the top make a difference? Gender proportions and the experiences of managerial and professional women. Human Relations, 49(8), 1093- 1105.

Cadinu, M., Maass, A., Rosabianca, A., & Kiesner, J. (2005). "Why do women underperform under stereotype threat?" American Psychological Society, 16(7).

Campbell, K., & Minguez-Vera, A. (2008). Gender Diversity in the boardroom and firm financial performance. Journal of Business Ethics, 83, 435-451.

Carli, L.I. & Eagly, A.H. (2001). "Gender, Hierarchy, and Leadership: An Introduction", Journal of social Issues, 57(4), 629-636.

Carlson, D.S., Kacmar, K.M. & Whitten, D. (2006). What men think they know about executive women, Harvard Business Review, September.

Carter, N.M. & Silva, C. (2010). Pipeline's broken promise. Catalyst: New York.

Cassells (2010) The gender wage gap in Australia: What it costs us, why it's still here and will it ever go? NATSEM Downloaded from http://www.canberra. edu.au/centres/natsem/ publications, 21-10-10.

Catalyst (2004). "The Bottom Line: Connecting Corporate Performance and Gender Diversity". Catalyst.

Catalyst (2007). The double-bind dilemma for women in leadership: Damned if you do, doomed if you don't, Catalyst.

Catalyst (2009). Work-Life: Prevalance, utilization, and benefits. Catalyst: New York. Downloaded from http://www.catalyst.org/publication/238/ work-life-prevalence-utilization- and-benefits.

Catalyst (2010a). Campbell Soup Company – winning in the workplace, winning in the marketplace, winning with women. Downloaded from http://www.catalyst.org/publication/386/campbell-soup-companywinning-in-the-marketplace-winning-in-the-workplace-winning-with-women. 23-11-10.

Catalyst (2010b). CH2M Hill – Constructing pathways for women through inclusion Downloaded from http://www. catalyst.org/publication/287/ch2m-hillconstructing-pathways-for-women- through-inclusion. 23-11-10.

Catalyst (2010c). Deloitte LLP – The women's initiative: living the lattice. Downloaded from http://www.catalyst.org/publication/385/deloitte-llpthe-womens-initiative-living-the-lattice.23-11-10.

Catalyst (2010d). RBC – Client first transformation: Achieving business results and cultural revitalisation through diversity. Downloaded from http://www.catalyst.org/publication/384 /bcclient-first-transformation-achieving-business-results-and-cultural-revitalization-through- diversity. 23-11-10.

Catalyst (2010e). Sidley Austin Brown & Wood LLP – Strategies for success: an ongoing commitment to diversity. Downloaded from http://www.catalyst.org/publication/128/sidley- austin-brown-wood-llpstrategies-for-success-an-ongoing-commitment-to-diversity. 23-11-10.

Catalyst (2010f). Telstra Corporation Limited – Next generation gender diversity: accelerating change for women leaders. Downloaded from http://www.catalyst.org/publication/ 383/telstra- corporation-limitednext-generation-gender-diversity-accelerating-change-for-women-leaders. 23-11-10.

Catalyst (2010g). The Chubb Corporation – Reach up, reach out, reach down. Downloaded from http://www.catalyst.org/publication/109/
the-chubb-corporationreach-up-reach-out-and-reach- down. 23-11-10.

Chief Executive Women (2009). The business case for women as leaders. Chief Executive Women: Australia.

Chinchilla, N., León, C., Torres, E. & Canela, M.A. (2006). Career inhibitors and career enablers for executive women. Working paper No. 632 IESE International Center for Work and Family, May 2006.

Coffman, J. Gadiesh, O. & Miller, W (2010). The great disappearing act: Gender parity up the corporate ladder. Bain & Company.

Cross, C. & Armstrong, C. (2008). "Understanding the role of networks in collective learning processes: The experiences of women", Advances in Developing Human Resources, 10(4), 600-613.

Danaher, K. & Branscombe, N.R. (2010). "Maintaining the system with tokenism: Bolstering individual mobility beliefs and identification with a discriminatory organization." The British Journal of Psychology, 49, 343-362.

Dasgupta, N. (2004). "Implicit Ingroup Favoritism, Outgroup Favoritism, and Their Behavioral Manifestation", Social Justice Research, 17(2), 143-169.

Dasgupta, N., & Asgari, S. (2004). "Seeing is believing.", Journal of Experimental Social Psychology, 40, 642-658.

Davis, T. (2010). Diversity on boards and in senior management – what does it mean and where's the value? Keynote presentation to Leaders Edge Luncheon Series, Victoria 28th July 2010.

Dencker, J. C. (2008). Corporate Restructuring and Sex Differences in Managerial Promotion. American Sociological Review, 73(June), 455-476.

Desvaux, G. & Devillard, S. (2008). "Women Matter 2: Female leadership, a competitive edge for the future." McKinsey& Company.

Desvaux, G., Devillard-Hoellinger, S. & Baumgarten, P (2007). "Women Matter: Gender Diversity, a corporate performance driver." McKinsey & Company.

Desvaux, G., Devillard-Hoellinger, S. & Meaney, MC. (2008). "A Business Case for Women", McKinsey Quarterly, September.

Dezso, CL & Ross, DG (2008). "Girl Power: Female participation in top management and firm performance." Working Paper No. RHS-05-104.

http://ssrn.com/abstract=1088182.

Dieckman, A.B., Goodfriend, W., & Goodwin, S. (2009). Dynamic stereotypes of power: perceived change and stability in gender hierarchies, Sex Roles, 50(3/4), 201-215.

Dovidio, J.F. (2010). "On the nature of contemporary prejudice: The third wave", Journal of Social Issues, 57(4), 829-849.

Dovidio. J.F., Hewstone,M., Glick, P., & Esses, V.M. (2010). "Prejudice, Stereotyping and Discrimination: Theoretical and Empirical Overview", In The Sage Book of Prejudice, Stereotyping and Discrimination. Sage: London.

Duehr, E. & Bono, J.E. (2006). "Men, women, and managers: Are stereotypes finally changing?", Personnel Psychology, 59, 815-846.

Duguid, M. (2011). "Female tokens in high-prestige work groups: Catalysts or inhibitors of group diversification?" Organization Behavior, 116, 104-115.

Eagly, A.H. (2007). "Female Leadership Advantage and Disadvantage: Resolving the Contradictions", Psychology of Women Quarterly, 31, 1-12.

Eagly, A.H. & Carli, L.L. (2007a). Through the labyrinth: The truth about how women become leaders. Harvard Business School Press: Boston, Ma.

Eagly, A. H., & Carli, L. L. (2007b). Women and the Labyrinth of Leadership. Harvard Business Review, September, 63-71.

Eagly, A.H. & Johannesen-Schmidt, M.C. (2001). "The Leadership Styles of Men and Women", Journal of Social Issues, 57(4), 781-797.

Eagly, A.H., Johannesen-Schmidt, M.C. & van Engen, M.L. (2003). "Transformational, Transactional, and Laissez-Faire Leadership Styles: A Meta-Analysis Comparing Women and Men", Psychological Bulletin, 129(4), 569-591.

Ely, R.J. & Meyerson, D. (2008). "Unmasking manly men." Harvard Business Review, July-August, 20.

Ely, R.J., Meyerson, D.E., & Davidson, M.N. (2006). "Rethinking political correctness", Harvard Business Review, September, 79-87.

EEONA (2010). Looking for a paradigm shift: 2010 Market leader report on diversity and gender. Downloaded from: http://www.eeona.org/ADES_2010_Report_15_October_2010.pdf

EOWA (2010a). 2010 Finalists Summary of Achievements. EOWA Business Achievement Awards. Downloaded from http://www.catalyst.org/publication/128/

sidley-austin-brown-wood- llpstrategies-for-success-an-ongoing-commitment-to-diversity.

EOWA (2010b). Australian Census of Women in Leadership. Equal Opportunity for Women in the Workplace Agency, Australian Government.

EOWA (2010c). EOWA Media Section, 2010 Employer of Choice for Women Downloaded from

http://www.eowa.gov.au/EOWA_Employer_of_Choice_for_Women/
2010/Media_Contacts.asp.

EOWA (2008a). Australian Census of Women in Leadership. Equal Opportunity for
Women in the Workplace, Australian Government.

EOWA (2008b). Pay, power and position: Beyond the 2008 EOWA Australian
census of women in leadership. Equal Opportunity for Women in the
Workplace, Australian Government.

EOWA. (2008c). Agenda in the board room. Equal Opportunity for Women in the
Workplace, Australian Government.

EOWA (2007). KPMG Case Study 2007). Downloaded from
http://www.eowa.gov.au/Case_ Studies/_docs/2007_EOCFW/KPMG.pdf 4-
11-10.

EOWA (2006a). GM Holden Case Study. Downloaded from
http://www.eowa.gov.au/Case_ Studies/2006/GM%20Holden.pdf, 4-11-10.

EOWA (2006b). Westpac Organizational Profile. Downloaded from
http://www.eowa.gov.au/Case_ Studies/_docs/2006%20Case%20Studies/
Westpac%20Org%20Profile.pdf. 4-11-10.

EOWA (undated). Gender workplace statistics at a glance. Downloaded from
http://www.eowa.gov. au/Information_Centres/Resource_Centre/
EOWA_Publications/Gender_stats_at_a_glance.pdf 4-11-10

Farrell, K. A., & Hersch, P. L. (2005). Additions to corporate boards: the effect of
gender. Journal of Corporate Finance, 11, 85-106.

Fels, A. (2004). Do women lack ambition? Harvard Business Review, April, 50 – 60.

Fine, C. (2010). Delusions of Gender. Allen & Unwin: Crows Nest, NSW.

Fine, C. (2012). "Status Quota. Do mandatory gender quotas work?" The Monthly,
March.

Foldy, E.G., Rivard, P., & Buckley, T.R. (2009). "Power, safety, and learning in
racially diverse groups.", Academy of Management Learning & Education,
8(1), 25-41.

Francoeur, C., Labelle, R., & Sinclair-Desgagné, B. (2008). Gender diversity in
corporate governance and top management. Journal of Business Ethics, 81,
83-95.

Furst, S.A & Reeves, M. (2008). "Queens of the hill: Creative Destruction and the
emergence of executive leadership of women", The Leadership Quarterly, 19
(2008), 372-384.

Goodman, J. S., Fields, D. L., & Blum, T. C. (2003). Cracks in the glass ceiling: In
what kinds of organizations do women make it to the top? Group
Organization Management, 28(4), 475-501.

Guillaume, C. & Pochic, S (2007). What would you sacrifice? Access to top
management and the work-life balance, Gender, Work and Organization,
16(1), 14-36.

Hamel, S. A. (2009). "Exit, voice, and sensemaking following psychological contract violations: Women's responses to career advancement barriers", Journal of Business Communications, 46(2), 234-261.

Heilman, M.E. (2001). Description and Prescription: How gender stereotypes prevent women's ascent up the organizational ladder, Journal of Social Issues, 57(4), 657-674.

Heilman, M. E., & Okimoto, T. G. (2007). Why are women penalized for success at male tasks?: The implied communality deficit. Journal of Applied Psychology, 92(1), 81-92.

Homan, A.D., Hollenbeck, J.R., Humphrey, S.E., van Knippenberg, D., Ilgen, D.R., & van Kleef, G.A. (2008). "Facing differences with an open mind: Openness to experience, salience of intragroup differences, and performance of diverse work groups.", Academy of Management Journal, 51(6), 1204-1222.

Hopkins, M. M., & Bilimoria, D. (2007). Social and emotional competencies predicting success for male and female executives. Journal of Management Development, 27(1), 13-35.

Hopkins, M. M., O'Neil, D. A., Passarelli, A., & Bilimoria, D. (2008). Women's leadership development strategic practices for women and organizations. Consulting Psychology Journal, 60(4), 348-365.

Hoyt, C. L. (2005). The role leadership efficacy and stereotype activation in women's identification with leadership. Journal of Psychology & Organizational Studies, 11(4), 2-15.

Ibarra, H. Carter, N.M. & Silva, C. (2010). Why men still get more promotions than women, Harvard Business Review, September.

Ibarra, H., & Obodaru, O. (2009). Women and the vision thing. Harvard Business Review, January, 62-70.

Implicit Attitude Test. Downloaded from https://implicit.harvard.edu/implicit. 8th August 2011.

Insync Surveys (2010). The Insync Surveys Retention Review. Downloaded from http://www.insyncsurveys.com.au/

Jacobs, R. L., & McClelland, D. C. (1994). Moving up the corporate ladder: A longitudinal study of the leadership motive pattern and managerial success in women and men. Consulting Psychology Journal, 46(1), 32-41.

Jost, J.T., Banaji, M.R. & Nosek, B.A. (2004). "A Decade of System Justification Theory: Accumulated Evidence of Conscious and Unconscious Bolstering of the Status Quo". Political Psychology, 25(6). 881-919.

Joy, L. (2008). Advancing women leaders: The connection between women board directors and women corporate officers (Report): Catalyst.

Kahneman, D., Lovallo, D., & Siboney, O. (2011). "Before you make that big decision", Harvard Business Review, June, 50-60. Kang, E., Ding, D., & Charoenwong, C. (2009). Investor reaction to women directors. Journal of Business Research, 10, 1016.

Kanter, R. M. (1977). Some effects of proportion on group life: Skewed sex ratios and responses to token women. American Journal of Sociology, 82, 965-990.

Kolb, D. M. (2009). Too bad for the women or does it have to be? Gender and negotiation research over the past twenty-five years. Negotiation Journal, October, 515-531.

Konrad, A. M., Kramer, V., & Erkut, S. (2008). Critical Mass: The impact of three or more women on corporate boards. Organizational Dynamics, 37(2), 145-164.

Koonce, R. (2004). "Women-only Executive Development", TD, October, 78 -84.

Krishnan, H. A. (2008). What causes turnover among women on top management teams? Journal of Business Research, 62, 1181-1186.

Krishnan, H. A., & Park, D. (2005). A few good women on top management teams. Journal of Business Research, 58, 1712-1720.

Kulik, C. (2010). "Effectively managing a diverse workforce: is good diversity management just good management?" Downloaded from http://www.unisa.edu.au/knowledgeworks /lectures/2010/kulik22june.asp. 10-7-10.

LeBlanc, R. (2009). More women on boards: what boards need, what shareholders want. Ivey Business Journal, 73(2).

Liff, S. & Ward, K. (2001). Distorted views through the glass ceiling: The construction of women's understandings of promotion and senior management positions, Gender, Work and Organization, 8(1), 19-36.

Liswood, L. (2010). The Loudest Duck: Moving beyond diversity while embracing differences to achieve success at work. John Wiley & Sons: New Jersey.

Lortie-Lusser, M. & Rinfret, N. (2002). The proportion of women managers: where is the critical mass? Journal of Applied Social Psychology, 32(9), 1974-1991.

Lyness, K. S., & Thompson, D. E. (1997). Above the glass ceiling: A comparison of matched samples of female and male executives. Journal of Applied Psychology, 82(3), 359-375.

Lyons, D. & McArthur, C (2007). "Gender's Unspoken Role in Leadership Evaluations", Human Resource Planning, 30(3), 24-32.

Matsa, D.A. & Miller, A.R. (2011). "A female style in corporate management? Evidence from quotas." http://ssrn.com/abstract=1636047

McCracken, D.M. (2000). Winning the talent war for women: sometimes it takes a revolution, Harvard Business Review, November-December.

Mavin, S. (2008). "Queen bees, wannabees and afraid to bees: No more 'best enemies' for women in management?", British Journal of Management, 19, S75-S84.

Metz, I. (2009). Organizational Factors, Social Factors, and Women's Advancement. Applied Psychology, 58(2), 193-213.

Murdoch, S (2010). Goldman to score managers on contribution to workplace diversity. The Australian, April 05 2001. Downloaded from http://www.theaustralian.com.au/ business/goldman-to-score-managers-on-contribution-to-workplace-diversity/story-e6frg8zx-1225849630074. 5-11-10.

Nesbit, P.L. & Seeger, T. (2007). The nature and impact of organizational activities to advance women in management in Australian firms, International Journal of Employment Studies, 15(1), 1-23.

Pace, A. (2009). Roaring all the way to the top. Training and Development, May, 16-17.

Phelan, J.A., Moss-Racusin, C.A. & Rudman, L.A. (2008). "Competent yet out in the cold: Shifting criteria for hiring reflect backlash toward agentic women." Psychology of Women Quarterly, 32, 406-413.

Prentice, D.A. & Carranza, E. (2002). "What Women and Men Should Be, Shouldn't Be, Are Allowed To Be, and Don't Have To Be: The Contents of Prescriptive Gender Stereotypes", Psychology of Women Quarterly, 26, 269-281.

Prime, J, Agin, M & Foust-Cummings, H (2010). Strategy Matters: Evaluating Company Approaches for Creating Inclusive Workplaces." Catalyst Report.

Prime, J. L., Carter, N. M., & Welbourne, T. M. (2009). Women "take care", men "take charge": Managers' stereotypic perceptions of women and men leaders. The Psychologist-Manager Journal, 12(1), 25-49.

Prime, J.L. & Moss-Racusin, C.A. (2009). Engaging men in gender initiatives: What change agents need to know. Catalyst Report: New York.

Reiby Institute (2010). "ASX500 Women Leaders." Research Report August 2010.

Reinhold, B. (2005). Smashing glass ceilings: Why women still find it tough to advance to the executive suite. Journal of Organizational Excellence, Summer, 43-55.

Rudman, L.A. & Glick, P (2008). The Social Psychology of Gender: How Power and Intimacy Shape Gender Relations. The Guilford Press: New York. Paperback edition 2010.

Sabattini, L. Warren, A., Dinolfo, S., Falk, E. & Castro, M (2010). Beyond generational differences: Bridging gender and generational diversity work. Catalyst: New York.

Sealy, R. (2010). Do the numbers matter? How senior women experience extreme gender-imbalance work environments. In Press, 1-40.

Singh, V. & Vinnicombe, S (2004). Why so few women directors in top UK boardrooms? Evidence and theoretical explanations, Corporate Governance: An International Review, 12(4), 479-488.

Smith, N., Smith, V. & Verner, M. (2005). Do women in top management affect firm performance? A panel study of 2500 Danish firms. IZA Discussion Paper No. 1708 August 2005.

Sools, A.M., Van Engen, M.L. & Baerveldt, C. (2007). "Gendered career-making practices: On 'doing ambition' or how managers discursively position themselves in a multinational corporation", Journal of Occupational and

Organizational Psychology, 80, 413-435.

Stanley, D., Phelps, E., & Banaji, M. (2008). "The neural basis of implicit attitudes", Current Directions in Psychological Science, 17(2), 164-169.

Summers, A. (2009). The other GFC: The gender fairness crisis. Address to Victorian Premier's Women's Summit, 8th September.

Syed, J. & Murray, P.A. (2008). "A Cultural Feminist Approach Towards Managing Diversity in Top Management Teams", Equal Opportunities International, 27(5), 413.432.

Tannen, D (1995). The power of talk: who gets heard and why, Harvard Business Review, September-October, 138-148.

Terjesen, S., Sealy, R., & Singh, V. (2009). Women directors on corporate boards: a review and research agenda. Corporate Governance: An International Review, 17(3), 320-337.

Tharenou, P. (2005). "Does mentor support increase women's career advancement more than men's? The differential effects of career and psychosocial support.", Australian Journal of Management, 30(1), 77-109.

The University of Melbourne (2007). Staff Equity and Diversity Framework 2008-2012.

Thiele, L.P. (2006). "The heart of judgement." Cambridge University Press: USA.

Unknown (2012). "Corrs named EOWA Employer of Choice for Women for Sixth Successive Year." Downloaded from www.cors.com.au/news/corrs-eowa-employer-of-choice-for-women-sixth-successive--year/.

Vinnicombe, S. & Singh, V. (2003). "Women-only Training: An essential part of women's leadership development", Journal of Change Management, 3(4), 294-306.

Warren, A.K. (2009). Cascading gender biases, compounding effects: An assessment of talent management systems. Catalyst: New York.

Wellington, S. Kropf, M.B. & Gerkovich, P.R. (2003). What's holding women back? Harvard Business Review, June.

WGEA (2015a). "All Roles Flex at Telstra." Downloaded from https://www.wgea.gov.au/2014-eocge-profiles/telstra-all-roles-flex-0 22-03-15.

WGEA (2015b). "Encouraging women into line roles." Downloaded from https://www.wgea.gov.au/2014-eocge-profiles/stockland-encouraging-women-pl-roles-0. 22-03-15.

WGEA (2015c). "Mirvac CEO a gender diversity champion." Downloaded from https://www.wgea.gov.au/2014-eocge-profiles/mirvac-ceo-gender-diversity-champio n. 22-03-15.

WGEA (2015d). "ANZ established Notable Women program." Downloaded from https://www.wgea.gov.au/2014-eocge-profiles/anz-notable-women-program-0. 22-03-15.

WGEA (2015e). "Norton Rose provides inclusive leadership training." Downloaded from https://www.wgea.gov.au/2014-eocge-profiles/norton-rose-fulbright-inclusive-leadership-training-0. 22-03-15.

Wilkinson, J., & Blackmore, J. (2009). Re-presenting women and leadership: A methodological journey. International Journal of Qualitative Studies in Education, 21(2), 123-136.

Wittenberg-Cox, E. (2010). How women mean business. Wiley: UK.

Woolley, A.W., Chabris, C.F., Pentland, A., Hashmi, N., & Malone, T.W. (2010). "Evidence for a Collective Intelligence Factor in the performance of human groups", Science, 330, 686-688.

www.ingramcontent.com/pod-product-compliance
Lightning Source LLC
Chambersburg PA
CBHW070722220326
41598CB00024BA/3264